My Little
Afternoon Tea
Book

More than 80
irresistible recipes

MURDOCH BOOKS

CONTENTS

LITTLE CAKES

Apple and coffee tea cakes

MAKES 8

185 g (6½ oz/1½ cups) plain (all-purpose) flour
1 teaspoon ground cinnamon
¼ teaspoon ground allspice
¾ teaspoon baking powder
¾ teaspoon bicarbonate of soda (baking soda)
125 ml (4 fl oz/½ cup) buttermilk
80 ml (2½ fl oz/⅓ cup) freshly made espresso coffee, cooled
185 g (6½ oz/¾ cup) unsalted butter, softened
140 g (5 oz/¾ cup) soft brown sugar
115 g (4 oz/½ cup) caster (superfine) sugar
2 teaspoons finely grated lemon zest
3 eggs
1 granny smith or golden delicious apple, peeled, cored and thinly sliced

STREUSEL TOPPING
¼ teaspoon ground allspice
45 g (1¾ oz/¼ cup) soft brown sugar
30 g (1 oz/¼ cup) plain (all-purpose) flour
60 g (2¼ oz/½ cup) chopped pecans
45 g (1¾ oz) unsalted butter, chilled and cut into cubes »

1 Preheat the oven to 180°C (350°F/Gas 4). Grease eight 6 x 8 cm (2½ x 3¼ inch) cake tins and line the base and sides of each tin with baking paper.

2 To make the streusel topping, place the allspice, sugar, flour and pecans in a small bowl and rub in the butter with your fingertips until the mixture resembles coarse breadcrumbs. Set aside.

3 Sift the flour, spices, baking powder and the bicarbonate of soda into a bowl and set aside. Combine buttermilk and coffee in a separate bowl.

4 Using electric beaters, cream butter and sugars in a third bowl until pale and fluffy, then stir in the zest. Add the eggs, one at a time, beating well after each addition. Fold in the flour mixture, alternately with the buttermilk mixture, stirring until just combined and smooth. Stir in the apple slices.

5 Spoon batter into the prepared tins and smooth the surface with the back of a spoon. Bake cakes for 10 minutes, then remove from the oven and sprinkle streusel mixture over the top. Return to the oven for a further 15 minutes or until golden brown and a skewer inserted in the centre of a cake comes out clean. Cool for 10 minutes in the tins, then transfer to wire racks to cool completely. Serve warm or at room temperature.

TIP Twelve smaller cakes can be made using 4 x 8 cm (1½ x 3¼ inch) tins. Bake for 20 minutes.

Rich dark chocolate cupcakes

MAKES 18

150 g (5½ oz) unsalted butter, chopped
200 g (7 oz) dark chocolate chips
185 g (6½ oz/1½ cups) self-raising flour
30 g (1 oz/¼ cup) unsweetened
cocoa powder
285 g (10 oz/1¼ cups) caster
(superfine) sugar
2 eggs, lightly beaten
chocolate curls, to decorate

CHOCOLATE TOPPING
250 g (9 oz) dark chocolate, chopped
40 g (1½ oz) unsalted butter

1 Preheat the oven to 160°C (315°F/Gas 2–3).
Line 18 standard muffin holes with paper cases.

2 Place the butter and chocolate chips in a small
heatproof bowl. Sit the bowl over a saucepan of
simmering water, making sure the bowl doesn't
touch the water. Stir the chocolate constantly until
it is melted. **»**

3 Sift flour and cocoa into a large bowl. Combine the melted butter and the chocolate mixture, sugar and egg, then add 185 ml (6 fl oz/¾ cup) of water and mix well. Add to the dry ingredients and stir until well combined. Divide mixture evenly among the cases. Bake for 20–25 minutes, or until a skewer comes out clean when inserted in the centre of a cake. Transfer onto a wire rack to cool.

4 To make the chocolate topping, place the chocolate and butter in a small heatproof bowl and sit it over a saucepan of simmering water, making sure the base of the bowl doesn't touch the water. Stir chocolate constantly until it melts. Decorate each cake with the topping and chocolate curls.

Pecan and orange cupcakes

MAKES 16 STANDARD OR 24 MINI CUPCAKES

125 g (4½ oz) unsalted butter, softened
170 g (6 oz/¾ cup) caster (superfine) sugar
2 eggs
100 g (3½ oz/¾ cup) ground pecans
3 teaspoons finely grated orange zest
185 g (6½ oz/1½ cups) self-raising
flour, sifted
125 ml (4 fl oz/½ cup) milk

CINNAMON ICING (FROSTING)
15 g (½ oz) unsalted butter, softened
¾ teaspoon ground cinnamon
185 g (6½ oz/1½ cups) icing (confectioners')
sugar, sifted

1 Preheat the oven to 180°C (350°F/Gas 4).
Line 16 standard (or 24 mini) muffin holes with
paper cases.

2 Beat butter and sugar with electric beaters until
pale and creamy. Gradually add eggs, one at a time,
beating well after each addition. Add the ground
pecans and orange zest, then use a metal spoon to
gently fold in the flour alternately with the milk. **»**

3 Divide mixture evenly among the cases. Bake for 50–60 minutes (40 minutes for minis), or until a skewer comes out clean when inserted in the centre of a cake. Leave in tin for 10 minutes, then transfer to a wire rack to cool.

4 To make icing, combine butter, icing sugar and cinnamon in a small bowl with 1½ tablespoons of hot water. Sit the bowl over a saucepan of simmering water, making sure the bowl doesn't touch the water, and then stir the icing until it is smooth and glossy. Remove from the heat and decorate each cake with icing.

Decadent double choc mousse cupcakes

MAKES 24

90 g (3¼ oz/¾ cup) plain (all-purpose) flour
30 g (1 oz/¼ cup) self-raising flour
125 g (4½ oz) unsalted butter, chopped
230 g (8½ oz/1 cup) caster (superfine) sugar
100 g (3½ oz) white chocolate, chopped
1 egg
1 teaspoon natural vanilla extract
125 ml (4 fl oz/½ cup) milk

CHOCOLATE MOUSSE
1 egg yolk
2 tablespoons caster (superfine) sugar
500 ml (17 fl oz/2 cups) cream,
375 g (13 oz) dark chocolate chips, melted
and cooled

1 Preheat the oven to 160°C (315°F/Gas 2–3).
Line 24 standard muffin holes with paper cases.

2 Sift the flours together in a bowl and make a well.
Place the butter, sugar and chocolate in a saucepan
and stir over low heat until the sugar has dissolved.
Remove from the heat and cool slightly. »

3 Whisk the egg, vanilla and milk until combined, then pour into the well in the flour, together with the chocolate mixture, and whisk to combine. Divide the mixture among the cases, until half-full. Bake for 15 minutes, or until a skewer comes out clean when inserted into the centre. Leave to cool completely on a wire rack.

4 To make the chocolate mousse, place the egg yolk and sugar in a small bowl and whisk over a small saucepan of simmering water until it becomes thick and creamy. Remove bowl from saucepan. Beat the cream in a bowl with electric beaters until soft peaks form. Add cooled melted chocolate and the egg mixture and continue to beat for 1–2 minutes, or until thickened and cooled.

5 Decorate the cakes with mousse, then place them on a tray and refrigerate for 1 hour, or until set.

Rhubarb yoghurt cupcakes

MAKES 24

150 g (5½ oz/1½ cups) finely sliced fresh
rhubarb, plus 24 extra pieces to decorate
310 g (11 oz/2½ cups) self-raising
flour, sifted
230 g (8½ oz/1 cup) caster (superfine) sugar
1 teaspoon natural vanilla extract
2 eggs, lightly beaten
125 g (4½ oz/½ cup) plain yoghurt
1 tablespoon rosewater
125 g (4½ oz) unsalted butter,
melted and cooled

1 Preheat the over to 180°C (350°F/Gas 4). Line
24 standard muffin holes with paper cases.

2 Combine the rhubarb, flour and sugar in a bowl.

3 Add the vanilla, egg, yoghurt, rosewater and the
melted butter, stirring with a wooden spoon until the
mixture is just combined.

4 Divide the mixture evenly among the cases, then
top each with a piece of extra rhubarb. Bake for
15 minutes, or until a skewer comes out clean when
inserted in the centre of a cake. Transfer to a wire
rack to cool.

Beehive cupcakes

MAKES 15

200 g (7 oz) unsalted butter, softened
185 g (6½ oz/1 cup) soft brown sugar
3 eggs
115 g (4 oz/⅓ cup) honey, warmed
280 g (10 oz/2¼ cups) self-raising
flour, sifted
15 chocolate-foil wrapped bumble bees
with wings

MARSHMALLOW ICING (FROSTING)
3 egg whites
330 g (11¾ oz/1½ cups) sugar
2 teaspoons light corn syrup
pinch of cream of tartar
1 teaspoon natural vanilla extract
yellow food colouring
15 toothpicks

1 Preheat the oven 180°C (350°F/Gas 4).
Line 15 standard muffin holes with paper cases.

2 Beat the butter and sugar with electric beaters
until light and creamy. Add eggs, one at a time,
beating well after each addition. Fold in the honey
and flour until combined. Divide the mixture evenly
amongthe cases. Bake for 18–20 minutes, or until a
skewer comes out clean when inserted in the centre
of a cake. Transfer to a wire rack to cool. »

3 To make the marshmallow icing, combine egg whites, sugar, corn syrup, cream of tartar and 100 ml (3½ fl oz) of water in a heatproof bowl. Sit the bowl over a saucepan of simmering water, making sure the bowl doesn't touch the water. Using electric beaters, beat for 5 minutes, or until the mixture is light and fluffy. Remove from heat. Add the vanilla and beat with electric beaters for 4–5 minutes, or until stiff peaks form. Add a little of the colouring, to tint to desired colour, and beat until just combined.

4 Spoon the icing into a piping bag fitted with a 1 cm (½ inch) round nozzle, and pipe the icing in circles on the cake tops to resemble a beehive. Push the pointy end of a toothpick into the base of each bumble bee and insert one into each cake.

Melt-and-mix chocolate cakes

MAKES 12

150 g (5½ oz) unsalted butter, cubed
230 g (8 oz/1 cup) soft brown sugar
185 ml (6 fl oz/¾ cup) freshly made
espresso coffee
2 eggs, at room temperature, lightly whisked
125 g (4½ oz/1 cup) self-raising flour
30 g (1 oz/¼ cup) plain (all-purpose) flour
60 g (2¼ oz/½ cup) unsweetened cocoa
powder
¼ teaspoon bicarbonate of soda
(baking soda)
icing (confectioners') sugar, sifted,
for dusting

CHOCOLATE BUTTER CREAM
250 g (9 oz/2 cups) icing (confectioners')
sugar, sifted
2 tablespoons unsweetened cocoa powder
60 g (2¼ oz/¼ cup) unsalted butter, softened
2 tablespoons hot water »

1 Preheat the oven to 180°C (350°F/Gas 4). Line a 12-hole standard muffin tin with paper cases.

2 Combine the butter, brown sugar and coffee in a saucepan over medium heat. Stir until the butter has melted and the sugar has dissolved. Remove from the heat and cool slightly.

3 Whisk the eggs into the butter mixture. In a separate bowl, sift together the flours, the cocoa and the bicarbonate of soda. Stir half the flour mixture into the butter mixture until just combined. Add the remaining flour mixture and stir until just combined. Transfer the mixture to a jug and pour into the prepared tin. Bake for 20 minutes, or until a skewer inserted in the centre of a cake comes out clean. Allow cakes to cool in the tin for 3 minutes, then transfer to a wire rack to cool completely.

4 To make butter cream, place 125 g (4½ oz/1 cup) of the sugar in a large bowl, add cocoa, butter and water and beat with electric beaters until smooth and creamy. Gradually add the remaining sugar and beat until the butter cream is thick.

5 Spread the butter cream over the cooled cakes using a spatula or flat-bladed knife.

6 The un-iced cakes will keep, stored in an airtight container, for up to 5 days. Iced cakes will keep in the same way for up to 2 days.

Apple pecan cupcakes

MAKES 16

310 g (11 oz/2½ cups) self-raising flour
1½ teaspoons ground cinnamon
165 g (5¾ oz/¾ cup) caster (superfine) sugar
2 granny smith apples (about 340 g/11¾ oz),
peeled, cored and coarsely grated
50 g (1¾ oz/½ cup) pecans, chopped
2 eggs, lightly beaten
125 ml (4 fl oz/½ cup) milk
15 g (½ oz) unsalted butter, melted
thick (double/heavy) cream or yoghurt,
to serve (optional)

1 Preheat the oven to 180°C (350°F/Gas 4).
Line 16 standard muffin holes with paper cases.

2 Combine flour, cinnamon, sugar, apple and pecans
in a bowl. Add egg, milk and melted butter, stirring
until the mixture is just combined and smooth.

3 Divide the mixture evenly among the cases. Bake
for 18–20 minutes, or until a skewer comes out clean
when inserted in the centre of a cake. Transfer to a
wire rack to cool.

4 If desired, serve with thick cream or yoghurt.

Sour cream and coffee walnut cakes

MAKES 10

60 g (2¼ oz/⅓ cup) soft brown sugar
75 g (2¾ oz/¾ cup) walnut halves, plus
10 extra, to decorate
1 teaspoon finely ground espresso
coffee beans
1 teaspoon ground cinnamon
115 g (4 oz) unsalted butter, softened
115 g (4 oz/½ cup) caster (superfine) sugar
2 eggs
185 g (6½ oz/1½ cups) plain
(all-purpose) flour
¾ teaspoon baking powder
½ teaspoon bicarbonate of soda
(baking soda)
225 g (8 oz) sour cream

ICING (FROSTING)
155 g (5½ oz/1¼ cups) icing (confectioners')
sugar, sifted
2–3 teaspoons freshly made strong
espresso coffee

1 Preheat the oven to 180°C (350°F/Gas 4). Grease
10 friand tins and line the bases with baking paper.**»**

2 Place the brown sugar, walnuts, ground coffee and cinnamon in the bowl of a food processor and pulse until the mixture resembles coarse breadcrumbs. Add 40 g (1½ oz) of butter and process until well combined. Set aside.

3 Cream remaining butter and the caster sugar in a bowl using electric beaters until pale and fluffy.

4 Add eggs, one at a time, beating well after each addition. Sift flour, baking powder and bicarbonate of soda into a separate bowl. Stir one-third of the flour mixture, then one-third of the sour cream, into the egg mixture, and continue alternating until all the flour mixture and the sour cream is incorporated and the mixture well combined.

5 Spoon half the batter into the prepared tins and spread across the base. Sprinkle reserved walnut mixture over the batter, then spoon on remaining batter to cover evenly. Bake for 20–25 minutes, or until lightly golden and a skewer inserted in the centre of a cake comes out clean. Set aside to cool slightly in the tins, then turn out onto a wire rack to cool completely.

6 To make the icing, place the sugar in a bowl and stir in enough coffee, adding a little water if necessary, to make a smooth, spreadable consistency.

7 Spread the icing over the cakes and place an extra walnut half on top. Allow icing to set before serving.

Fruit tart cupcakes

MAKES 12

85 g (6½ oz) unsalted butter, softened
170 g (6 oz/¾ cup) caster (superfine) sugar
1 teaspoon natural vanilla extract
3 eggs
125 g (4½ oz/1 cup) self-raising flour
30 g (1 oz/¼ cup) plain (all-purpose) flour
125 ml (4 fl oz/½ cup) milk
125 g (4½ oz/½ cup) purchased
thick custard
1 kiwi fruit, peeled, halved
and sliced
125 g (5 oz) strawberries, hulled
and sliced
6 red grapes, halved
160 g (5⅔ oz/½ cup) apricot jam

1 Preheat the oven to 180°C (350°F/Gas 4).
Line 12 standard muffin holes with paper cases.

2 Beat the butter, sugar and vanilla together with
electric beaters until light and creamy. Add eggs,
one at a time, beating well after each addition. Sift
flours together and fold in alternately with the milk. **»**

3 Divide the mixture evenly among the cases and bake for 15 minutes, or until a skewer comes out clean when inserted in the centre of a cake. Transfer to a wire rack to cool.

4 Cut a hole in the centre of each cake, leaving a 1 cm (½ inch) border. Fill each cavity with 2 teaspoons of custard. Arrange the fruit over the custard. Heat the jam until runny. Lightly brush the jam over the top of each cake. Refrigerate. Stand at room temperature for 15 minutes before serving.

Lavender and honey madeleines

MAKES 30

30 g (1 oz) unsalted butter
2 teaspoons honey
2½ tablespoons caster (superfine) sugar
½ teaspoon dried lavender
30 g (1 oz/¼ cup) plain (all-purpose) flour
1½ tablespoons ground almonds
1 large egg, at room temperature
1 tablespoon icing (confectioners') sugar,
sifted, for dusting (optional)

1 Preheat oven to 180°C (350°F/Gas 4). Lightly grease 30 mini madeleine moulds.

2 Melt butter and honey in a small saucepan over a medium heat. Set aside to cool. Place caster sugar and the lavender in the bowl of a food processor and process until combined. Sift the flour, the ground almonds and a pinch of salt three times onto baking paper. (This will lighten the madeleines' texture.) »

3 Beat the egg and sugar mixture in a bowl with electric beaters until thick and creamy. Add flour mixture and the cooled butter mixture and fold in lightly with a metal spoon until just combined. Allow to stand for 10 minutes.

4 Spoon into prepared madeleine moulds until three-quarters full. Bake for 6–8 minutes, or until lightly golden. Carefully remove from the moulds and place on a wire rack to cool. Dust lightly with icing sugar before serving.

5 Madeleines should be eaten the same day that they are baked.

Marble cupcakes

MAKES 10

85 g (6½ oz) unsalted butter, softened
170 g (6 oz/¾ cup) caster (superfine) sugar
1 teaspoon natural vanilla extract
3 eggs
125 g (4½ oz/1 cup) self-raising flour
30 g (1 oz/¼ cup) plain (all-purpose) flour
125 ml (4 fl oz/½ cup) milk
pink food colouring
2 tablespoons unsweetened cocoa
powder, sifted

MARBLE ICING (FROSTING)
280 g (10 oz/2¼ cups) icing (confectioners')
sugar, sifted
100 g (3½ oz) unsalted butter, softened
pink food colouring

1 Preheat the oven to 180°C (350°F/Gas 4).
Line 10 standard muffin holes with paper cases.

2 Beat butter, sugar and vanilla together with
electric beaters until light and creamy. Add eggs,
one at a time, beating well after each addition. Sift
flours together and fold in alternately with milk. »

3 Divide mixture into three equal portions. Add a few drops of pink food colouring to one portion and mix to combine. Add the cocoa to another portion and mix to combine. Divide the three colours evenly into each case and gently swirl the mixture with a skewer. Bake for 15 minutes, or until a skewer comes out clean when inserted in the centre of a cake. Transfer onto a wire rack to cool.

4 To make the marble icing, mix the icing sugar, butter and sufficient hot water to make a spreadable icing. Spread the icing over each cake. Dip a skewer in pink food colouring and swirl it through the icing to create a marbled effect.

Butterfly cupcakes

MAKES 12

120 g (4¼ oz) unsalted butter, softened
145 g (5 oz/⅔ cup) caster (superfine) sugar
185 g (6½ oz/1½ cups) self-raising flour
125 ml (4 fl oz/½ cup) milk
2 eggs
125 ml (4 fl oz/½ cup) thick (double/heavy) cream
80 g (1½ oz/¼ cup) strawberry jam
icing (confectioners') sugar, to sprinkle

1 Preheat the oven to 180°C (350°F/Gas 4). Line 12 standard muffin holes with paper cases.

2 Beat the butter, sugar, flour, milk and eggs with electric beaters on low speed until combined. Increase to medium speed and beat until mixture is smooth and pale. Divide mixture evenly among the cases and bake for 15–20 minutes, or until a skewer comes out clean when inserted in the centre of a cake. Transfer to a wire rack to cool.

3 Cut a shallow round from the centre of each cake using the point of a sharp knife, then cut the round in half. Spoon 2 teaspoons of cream into the cavity of each cake, then top with 1 teaspoon of jam. Position the two halves of the cake round in the jam to make butterfly wings. Sprinkle with sifted icing sugar.

Apricot, sour cream and coconut cupcakes

MAKES 20

220 g (7¾ oz/1¾ cups) self-raising flour
45 g (1⅔ oz/½ cup) desiccated coconut
125 g (4½ oz) unsalted butter
230 g (8½ oz/1 cup) caster (superfine) sugar
2 eggs, lightly beaten
250 ml (9 fl oz/1 cup) apricot nectar
125 g (4½ oz/½ cup) sour cream
825 g (1 lb 13 oz) tinned apricot halves in juice,
drained (you need 20 apricot halves)
80 g (2¾ oz/¼ cup) apricot jam

1 Preheat the oven to 180°C (350°F/Gas 4).
Line 20 standard muffin holes with paper cases.

2 Sift the flour into a large mixing bowl, then add
coconut and make a well in the centre. Melt butter
and sugar in a small saucepan over low heat, stirring
until the sugar has dissolved. Remove from the heat.
Whisk the combined egg and apricot nectar into the
sour cream. Add both the butter and egg mixtures to
the well in the dry ingredients and then stir with a
wooden spoon until combined. »

3 Divide mixture evenly among the cases and place an apricot half, cut side up, on the top of each cake. Bake for 18–20 minutes, or until a skewer comes out clean when inserted into a cake. Transfer to a wire rack to cool.

4 Heat the jam in a small saucepan over a gentle heat until melted. Brush a little jam over each cake.

Apple and raisin cupcakes

MAKES 12

185 g (6½ oz/1½ cups) self-raising flour
150 g (5½ oz) unsalted butter, chopped
140 g (5 oz/¾ cup) soft brown sugar
125 g (4½ oz/1 cup) raisins, plus extra
to decorate
120 g (4¼ oz) apple purée
3 eggs, lightly beaten

YOGHURT TOPPING
250 g (9 oz/1 cup) plain yoghurt
1 tablespoon soft brown sugar

1 Preheat the oven to 180°C (350°F/Gas 4).
Line 12 standard muffin holes with paper cases.

2 Sift the flour into a large bowl and make a well
in the centre. Melt the butter and sugar in a small
saucepan over a low heat, stirring until the sugar
has dissolved. Remove from the heat. Combine the
raisins and apple purée with the butter mixture.
Pour into the well in the flour, along with the egg.
Stir with a wooden spoon until combined. **»**

3 Divide mixture evenly among the cases. Bake for 15 minutes, or until a skewer comes out clean when inserted in the centre of a cake. Transfer to a wire rack to cool completely.

4 To make the yoghurt topping, combine the yoghurt and the sugar. Spread 1 tablespoon of topping over each cake.

SLICES

Cider crumble slice

MAKES 24 PIECES

20 g (¾ oz) unsalted butter
1½ tablespoons golden syrup (light treacle)
150 ml (5 fl oz) alcoholic apple cider
250 g (9 oz/2 cups) self-raising flour
pinch of ground ginger
45 g (1/⅔ oz/¼ cup) soft brown sugar
75 g (2½ oz) pitted dates, chopped
75 g (2½ oz/¾ cup) walnut halves, chopped
1 egg

TOPPING
1 large granny smith apple
40 g (1½ oz) unsalted butter
2½ tablespoons caster (superfine) sugar
60 g (2¼ oz/½ cup) plain (all-purpose) flour
75 g (2½ oz/¾ cup) walnut halves, chopped

1 Preheat the oven to 170°C (325°F/Gas 3).
Lightly grease a 20 x 30 cm (8 x 12 inch) baking tin
and line the base with baking paper, extending the
paper over two long sides for easy removal later.

2 Melt butter and golden syrup in a saucepan over
low heat. Remove from heat and stir in the cider. »

3 Sift flour and ginger into a medium bowl. Stir in the sugar, dates and walnuts. Add the golden syrup mixture and the egg and beat until smooth. Spoon into the prepared tin and smooth the surface with a spatula.

4 To make the topping, peel, core and thinly slice the apple, then cut into 1.5 cm (⅝ inch) pieces. Melt the butter in a small saucepan, add the sugar, flour, apple and walnuts, stirring well. Spread over the base. Bake for 30 minutes,

Choc mallow bars

30 g (1 oz/¼ cup) icing (confectioners') sugar
150 g (5½ oz) unsalted butter, melted
1 egg
160 g (5¾ oz/½ cup) raspberry jam,
slightly warmed
250 g (9 oz/2¾ cups) white marshmallows
80 ml (2½ fl oz/⅓ cup) cream
160 g (5¾ oz/1 cup) chopped
unsalted peanuts
200 g (7 oz) milk chocolate, chopped
2 teaspoons vegetable oil

1 Preheat the oven to 200°C (400°F/Gas 6). Lightly grease a 16 x 26 cm (6¼ x 10½ inch) baking tin and line the base with baking paper, extending the paper over the long sides for easy removal later.

2 Sift the flour, sugar and a pinch of salt into a large bowl. Add the butter and the egg, and mix well to combine. Press the dough into the prepared tin and refrigerate for 20 minutes. Transfer to the oven to bake for 20 minutes. Remove from the oven and allow to cool. Spread the jam over the base. **»**

3 Place the marshmallows and the cream in a saucepan. Stir over low heat for 5 minutes, or until the marshmallows have melted. Pour over the base. Sprinkle the peanuts over the top.

4 Place chocolate in a heatproof bowl. Half-fill a saucepan with water, bring to the boil and then remove from the heat. Place the bowl over the saucepan, ensuring the base of the bowl doesn't touch the water. Stand, stirring occasionally, until the chocolate has melted. Stir in the oil and cool slightly. Pour chocolate evenly over the top of slice and refrigerate until set. Cut into fingers and serve.

Peach and sour cream slice

MAKES 15 PIECES

150 g (5½ oz) unsalted butter, softened
115 g (4 oz/½ cup) caster (superfine) sugar
1 teaspoon natural vanilla extract
3 eggs
155 g (5½ oz/1¼ cups) self-raising
flour, sifted
125 ml (4 fl oz/½ cup) milk
45 g (1⅔ oz/½ cup) desiccated coconut
½ teaspoon ground cardamom
300 g (10½ oz) sour cream
6 fresh peaches, peeled and sliced,
or 2 x 410 g (14½ oz) tins peach slices,
drained and patted dry
75 g (2½ oz/⅓ cup) raw (demerara) sugar

1 Preheat the oven to 170°C (325°F/Gas 3).
Lightly grease a 16 x 26 cm (6¼ x 10½ inch) baking
tin and line base with baking paper, extending the
paper over the long sides for easy removal later. **»**

2 Cream the butter, caster sugar and vanilla in a large bowl using electric beaters until pale and fluffy. Add two of the eggs, one at a time, beating well after each addition. Fold in the flour and milk, in batches, alternating between the two. Fold in coconut and cardamom. Use a spatula to spread mixture into the prepared tin. Bake for 20 minutes, or until a skewer inserted in the centre comes out clean. Allow to cool slightly.

3 Meanwhile, increase the oven temperature to 200°C (400°F/Gas 6). Mix the sour cream and the remaining egg in a small bowl and spread over the cooked base. Arrange the peaches over the filling. Sprinkle with raw sugar and bake for 30–40 minutes, or until golden and set on top. Allow to cool in the tin before slicing into fingers.

Snickerdoodle slice

MAKES 20 PIECES

2 eggs
250 ml (9 fl oz/1 cup) milk
250 g (9 oz/2 cups) plain (all-purpose) flour
230 g (8¼ oz/1 cup) caster (superfine) sugar
1 tablespoon ground cinnamon
2 teaspoons baking powder
125 g (4½ oz/½ cup) unsalted butter, melted
thick (double/heavy) cream, to
serve (optional)

CINNAMON SUGAR
3 tablespoons sugar
3 teaspoons ground cinnamon

1 Preheat the oven to 180°C (350°F/Gas 4).
Lightly grease a 20 x 30 cm (8 x 12 inch) baking tin
and line the base with baking paper, extending the
paper over two long sides for easy removal later.

2 Place eggs and milk in a small bowl and whisk to
combine. Sift the flour, sugar, cinnamon and baking
powder into a large bowl. Make a well in the centre,
pour in the egg mixture and stir with a metal spoon
to roughly combine. Fold in butter until smooth—do
not overmix. Spoon half the dough into the prepared
tin and smooth the surface with a spatula. »

3 To make the cinnamon sugar, combine the sugar and cinnamon in a small bowl and mix well.

4 Sprinkle two-thirds of the cinnamon sugar over the dough in the tin. Gently spoon the remaining dough over the top and smooth the surface. Dust with the remaining cinnamon sugar. Bake for 25–30 minutes, or until firm. Cool in the tin for 20 minutes, then lift onto a wire rack to cool completely. Cut into pieces and serve with the cream, if desired.

Raspberry mascarpone trifle slice

MAKES 12 PIECES

375 g (13 oz) jam rollettes
60 ml (2 fl oz/¼ cup) amaretto
125 g (4½ oz) mascarpone cheese
80 g (2¾ oz/⅓ cup) caster (superfine) sugar
2 eggs, separated
200 g (7 oz) white chocolate, grated
300 g (10½ oz) raspberries
thick (double/heavy) cream, to
serve (optional)

1 Lightly grease a 16 x 26 cm (6¼ x 10½ inch) baking tin and line the base and the sides with baking paper.

2 Slice each rollette into four thin rounds. Place slices, cut-side-down, close together in the prepared tin. Press down lightly to ensure base of tin is covered. Sprinkle over the amaretto.

3 Place the mascarpone, sugar and egg yolks in a medium bowl and mix to combine—do not overmix. Beat egg whites in a separate bowl until soft peaks form. Fold the egg whites and chocolate into the mascarpone mixture using a large metal spoon. Spread onto the base and smooth the surface with a spatula. Cover and place in the refrigerator for 2 hours, or until firm. Decorate with the raspberries. Cut into pieces and serve with cream, if desired.

Classic brownies

MAKES 16 PIECES

125 g (4½ oz) dark chocolate, chopped
90 g (3¼ oz/⅓ cup) unsalted butter, softened
230 g (8¼ oz/1 cup) caster (superfine) sugar
1 teaspoon natural vanilla extract
2 eggs
85 g (3 oz/⅔ cup) plain (all-purpose)
flour, sifted
30 g (1 oz/¼ cup) unsweetened cocoa
powder, sifted
½ teaspoon baking powder, sifted
icing (confectioners') sugar, for dusting

1 Preheat the oven to 180°C (350°F/Gas 4). Grease a
17 cm (6½ inch) square baking tin and line the base
with baking paper, extending the paper over two
opposite sides for easy removal later.

2 Place the chocolate in a heatproof bowl. Half-fill a
saucepan with water, bring to the boil and remove
from the heat. Place the bowl over the saucepan,
ensuring the base of the bowl doesn't touch the
water. Stir occasionally until chocolate has melted.
Cool slightly. »

3 Cream butter, sugar and vanilla in a medium bowl with electric beaters until pale and fluffy. Add the eggs, one at a time, beating well after each addition. Stir in the chocolate.

4 Fold in the combined flour, cocoa and baking powder with a metal spoon. Pour into the prepared tin and smooth the surface with a spatula. Bake for 30–35 minutes, or until firm to touch and the sides come away from the tin easily. Cool in tin. Remove, cut into squares and serve, dusted with icing sugar.

Macadamia fingers

MAKES 18 PIECES

180 g (6¼ oz) unsalted butter, softened
1 teaspoon natural vanilla extract
80 g (2¾ oz/⅓ cup) caster (superfine) sugar
250 g (9 oz/2 cups) plain (all-purpose)
flour, sifted

TOPPING
125 g (4½ oz/½ cup) unsalted butter
2 x 400 g (14 oz) tins condensed milk
2 tablespoons golden syrup (light treacle)
200 g (7 oz/1¼ cups) macadamia nuts,
coarsely chopped

1 Preheat the oven to 180°C (350°F/Gas 4). Lightly grease a 20 x 30 cm (8 x 12 inch) baking tin and line the base and sides with baking paper, extending the paper over the long sides for easy removal later.

2 Place the butter, vanilla and sugar in a large bowl and cream with electric beaters until pale and fluffy. Stir in the flour and mix until well combined. Press the mixture firmly into the prepared tin and bake for 25 minutes, or until the base is cooked and a little browned. Cool slightly. **»**

3 To make topping, place butter, condensed milk and golden syrup in a saucepan and stir over low heat until the butter has melted. Increase the heat to medium and stir constantly for 15–20 minutes, or until the mixture is thick and caramel-like. Add the macadamias and pour onto biscuit base. Bake for 10 minutes, or until golden.

4 Cool in the tin. Remove from the tin, cut in half lengthways, then cut into fingers and serve.

Fig and cinnamon slice

MAKES 15 PIECES

125 g (4½ oz/½ cup) unsalted butter,
softened
55 g (2 oz) soft brown sugar
1 teaspoon ground cinnamon
185 g (6½ oz/1½ cups) plain (all-purpose)
flour, sifted
375 g (13 oz) dried figs
1 cinnamon stick
115 g (4 oz/½ cup) caster (superfine) sugar
375 ml (13 fl oz/1½ cups) boiling water

1 Preheat the oven to 180°C (350°F/Gas 4).
Lightly grease an 18 x 28 cm (7 x 11¼ inch) baking
tin and line the base with baking paper, extending
the paper over the long sides for easy removal later.

2 Beat butter, brown sugar and ground cinnamon in
a medium bowl with electric beaters until light and
fluffy. Fold in the flour with a large metal spoon.
Press the mixture evenly into the prepared tin and
bake for 25 minutes. Cool slightly. **»**

3 Combine figs, cinnamon stick, caster sugar and water in a saucepan and bring to the boil. Reduce the heat and simmer for 20 minutes, or until the figs have softened and the liquid has reduced by one-third. Remove the cinnamon stick and place the mixture in the bowl of a food processor. Process in short bursts until smooth.

4 Pour the hot fig mixture onto the cooked base and bake for 10 minutes, or until set. Cool in the tin and when cold, lift out and cut into squares.

Ginger cheesecake slice

MAKES 24 PIECES

BASE
200 g (7 oz) ginger-flavoured biscuits
(cookies), finely crushed
60 g (2¼ oz/¼ cup) unsalted butter, melted
½ teaspoon ground cinnamon

FILLING
500 g (1 lb 2 oz/2 cups) cream cheese, at
room temperature
175 g (6 oz/½ cup) golden syrup
(light treacle)
2 tablespoons caster (superfine) sugar
2 eggs, lightly beaten
55 g (2 oz/¼ cup) finely chopped
crystallised ginger
125 ml (4 fl oz/½ cup) cream, lightly whipped

TOPPING
125 ml (4 fl oz/½ cup) cream
2 teaspoons caster (superfine) sugar
55 g (2 oz/¼ cup) thinly sliced
crystallised ginger

1 Preheat the oven to 170°C (325°F/Gas 3).
Lightly grease a 20 x 30 cm (8 x 12 inch) baking
tin and line the base with bakin tin. »

2 To make the base, combine the biscuits, butter and cinnamon in a bowl and mix well. Press into the prepared tin. Refrigerate for 30 minutes, or until firm.

3 To make the filling, beat the cream cheese, golden syrup and sugar in a medium bowl using electric beaters until light and fluffy. Add the eggs, one at a time, beating well after each addition. Fold in ginger and whipped cream. Spread over the base and bake for 25 minutes, or until it is just set. Turn off the oven, leave the door slightly ajar and cool in the oven. Remove from the tin when completely cool and trim the edges.

4 To make the topping, beat the cream and caster sugar in a large bowl using electric beaters until soft peaks form.

5 Spread topping over the trimmed cheesecake using a spatula. Use a hot dry knife to cut the cheesecake into three strips lengthways and then cut each strip into eight pieces. Decorate with the ginger and serve.

Chestnut cream slice

MAKES 16 PIECES

CHOCOLATE SPONGES
80 g (2¾ oz) self-raising flour
60 g (2¼ oz/½ cup) plain (all-purpose) flour
1 tablespoon unsweetened cocoa powder
110 g (3¾ oz) caster (superfine) sugar
2 eggs, lightly beaten
2 teaspoons natural vanilla extract
120 g (4¼ oz/½ cup) unsalted butter,
softened
125 ml (4 fl oz/½ cup) milk
125 ml (4 fl oz/½ cup) brandy

BASE
60 g (2¼ oz/½ cup) plain (all-purpose) flour
2 tablespoons unsweetened cocoa powder
2 tablespoons caster (superfine) sugar
60 g (2¼ oz/¼ cup) unsalted butter, melted
1 tablespoon milk
½ teaspoon natural vanilla extract

CHESTNUT CREAM
30 g (1 oz) unsalted butter, softened
250 g (9 oz/1 cup) unsweetened
chestnut purée
60 g (2 oz/½ cup) icing (confectioner's) sugar
2 tablespoons brandy »

CHOCOLATE GLAZE
100 g (3 ½ oz) dark chocolate, chopped
60 g (2 oz/ ¼ cup) unsalted butter, chopped
1 tablespoon cream

1 Preheat oven to 180°C (350°F/Gas 4). Grease two 17 cm (6½ inch) square baking tins and line the bases and sides with baking paper.

2 To make the chocolate sponges, sift the flours and the cocoa into a large bowl, stir in sugar and make a well in the centre. Combine the egg, vanilla extract, butter and milk in a separate bowl, pour into the well and stir until just combined. Divide evenly between the prepared tins and bake for 10–15 minutes, or until the top springs back on each cake when lightly touched. Set aside to cool for 5 minutes, then turn out onto wire racks to cool completely. Brush the top of each cake with the brandy.

3 Increase the oven temperature to 190°C (375°F/Gas 5). Lightly grease a 17 cm (6½ inch) square baking tin. Line the base of the baking tin with baking paper, extending the paper over the two opposite sides for easy removal later. **»**

4 To make the base, sift the flour, cocoa and sugar into a bowl. Add the butter, milk and vanilla and mix until well combined. Press into the prepared tin and smooth the top with the back of a spoon. Refrigerate for 20 minutes. Cover the dough with baking paper, fill with baking beads or uncooked rice and bake for 10–15 minutes, or until dry. Remove the paper and weights. Reduce the oven temperature to 180°C (350°F/Gas 4) and bake for 8–10 minutes, or until deep brown. Leave to cool.

5 To make the chestnut cream, beat the butter, chestnut purée, sugar and brandy in a bowl using electric beaters until smooth.

6 Spread half the chestnut cream over the cooled base and place one layer of chocolate sponge on the top, pressing down gently. Repeat with the remaining chestnut cream and chocolate sponge.

7 To make the chocolate glaze, place chocolate, butter and cream in a heatproof bowl. Half-fill a saucepan with water, bring to the boil and remove from the heat. Place the bowl over the saucepan, making sure the base of the bowl doesn't touch the water. Stir occasionally until chocolate and butter have melted. Stir until smooth and well combined. Set aside to cool.

8 Spread the chocolate glaze over the slice and leave to set. Cut into pieces and serve.

Semolina syrup slice

MAKES 16 PIECES

300 g (10½ oz/2½ cups) coarse semolina
1 teaspoon bicarbonate of soda
(baking soda)
250 ml (9 fl oz/1 cup) milk
250 g (9 oz/1 cup) plain yoghurt
125 g (4½ oz/½ cup) unsalted butter, melted
2 tablespoons honey
16 blanched almonds
460 g (1 lb ¼ oz/2 cups) caster
(superfine) sugar
500 ml (17 fl oz/2 cups) water
1 tablespoon lemon juice
1 tablespoon rosewater

1 Lightly grease a 16 x 26 cm (6¼ x 10½ inch) baking
tin and line the base with baking paper, extending
the paper over the long sides for easy removal later.

2 Place the semolina and bicarbonate of soda in a
bowl and mix to combine. Whisk the milk, yoghurt,
butter and honey in a separate bowl. Quickly, stir
the milk mixture into the semolina mixture until
combined. Pour into the prepared tin, smooth the
top with a spatula and refrigerate for 30 minutes,
or until set. »

3 Preheat the oven to 180°C (350°F/Gas 4). Score the slice diagonally into diamond shapes. Top each diamond slice with an almond and then bake for 25–30 minutes, or until golden brown.

4 Meanwhile, place sugar and water in a saucepan. Cook, stirring occasionally, over low heat until the sugar has dissolved. Bring to the boil, reduce the heat to low and simmer for 15 minutes, or until the syrup is thick. Stir in lemon juice and rosewater and remove from the heat. Pour the syrup over the slice and cool in the tin. Cut into diamonds and serve.

Apple and berry slice

MAKES 16 PIECES

150 g (5½ oz) unsalted butter, softened
310 g (11 oz/1⅓ cups) caster (superfine)
sugar
2 eggs
170 ml (5½ fl oz/⅔ cup) buttermilk
1 teaspoon natural vanilla extract
250 g (9 oz/2 cups) self-raising flour, sifted
2 large apples, peeled, cored and
thinly sliced
150 g (5½ oz) blueberries
150 g (5½ oz) blackberries
icing (confectioners') sugar, sifted, for
dusting (optional)

1 Preheat the oven to 180°C (350°F/Gas 4).
Lightly grease a 20 x 30 cm (8 x 12 inch) baking tin
and line the base with baking paper, extending the
paper over two long sides for easy removal later. **»**

2 Cream the butter and sugar in a large bowl using electric beaters until pale and fluffy. Add the eggs, one at a time, beating well after each addition. In a separate bowl, combine the buttermilk and vanilla. Alternately stir in flour and the buttermilk mixture. Mix until smooth. Spread a 5 mm (¼ inch) layer in the prepared tin.

3 Arrange the apple on the base. Spoon remaining mixture over the apple, smooth the surface with a spatula and scatter the berries over top. Bake on the middle shelf in the oven for 40 minutes, or until cooked and golden. Cool in the tin for 30 minutes before lifting onto a wire rack to cool completely. Dust with icing sugar, if using, and then cut the slice into squares.

Rocky road slice

MAKES 15 PIECES

400 g (14 oz) white chocolate, chopped
250 g (9 oz/2¾ cups) pink and white
marshmallows, chopped
150 g (5½ oz) dried strawberries or Turkish
delight, roughly chopped
45 g (1⅔ oz/¾ cup) shredded
coconut, toasted
100 g (3½ oz) shortbread biscuits (cookies),
roughly chopped
400 g (14 oz) milk chocolate, chopped

1 Lightly grease a 16 x 26 cm (6¼ x 10½ inch) baking
tin and line the base with baking paper, extending
the paper over the long sides for easy removal later.

2 Place the white chocolate in a heatproof bowl.
Half-fill a saucepan with water, bring to the boil and
remove from the heat. Sit bowl over the saucepan,
making sure the base of the bowl doesn't touch the
water. Stir occasionally until chocolate has melted.
Cool slightly. Pour into the tin. »

3 Sprinkle the marshmallow pieces, strawberries or Turkish delight, coconut and biscuit pieces over the chocolate base.

4 Melt the milk chocolate in a heatproof bowl over a saucepan of just-boiled water, making sure the base of the bowl doesn't touch the water. Cool slightly. Pour over the base and filling, then refrigerate until set. Cut into squares and serve.

Peanut toffee shortbread

MAKES 18 PIECES

290 g (10¼ oz) unsalted butter, softened
115 g (4 oz/½ cup) caster (superfine) sugar
1 egg
185 g (6½ oz/1½ cups) plain (all-purpose) flour, sifted
60 g (2¼ oz/½ cup) self-raising flour, sifted
185 g (6½ oz/1 cup) soft brown sugar
2 tablespoons golden syrup (light treacle)
½ teaspoon lemon juice
400 g (14 oz/2½ cups) toasted unsalted peanuts

1 Preheat the oven to 180°C (350°F/Gas 4). Lightly grease an 18 x 28 cm (7 x 11¼ inch) baking tin and line the base and sides with baking paper, extending the paper over the long sides for easy removal later.

2 Place 110 g (3¾ oz) of the butter and all the caster sugar in a large bowl and cream with electric beaters until pale and fluffy. Add the egg and beat well. Fold in the sifted flours with a large metal spoon until just combined. Press into tin and bake for 15 minutes, or until firm and lightly coloured. Cool for 10 minutes. »

3 Place brown sugar, golden syrup, lemon juice and the remaining butter in a saucepan and stir over low heat until the sugar has dissolved. Simmer, stirring occasionally, for a further 5 minutes. Add peanuts and mix well.

4 Spread the peanut toffee topping evenly over the base using two spoons, being careful as the mixture is very hot. Bake for 5 minutes, or until golden. Leave to slightly cool in the tin for 15 minutes, then turn out and cut into fingers while still warm.

Old English matrimonials

200 g (7 oz/2 cups) quick-cooking rolled
(porridge) oats
220 g (7¾ oz/1¾ cups) plain
(all-purpose) flour
230 g (8¼ oz/1¼ cups) soft brown sugar
250 g (9 oz/1 cup) unsalted butter, melted
90 g (3¼ oz/1 cup) desiccated coconut
315 g (11 oz/1 cup) strawberry jam,
slightly warmed

1 Preheat the oven to 180°C (350°F/Gas 4).
Lightly grease a 16 x 26 cm (6¼ x 10½ inch) baking
tin and line the base with baking paper, extending
the paper over the long sides for easy removal later.

2 Combine the oats, flour, sugar, butter, salt, coconut
and a pinch of salt in a large bowl. Press half the oat
mixture into the prepared tin. Spread the jam on top.
Sprinkle over the remaining oat mixture and press
lightly with your fingertips to flatten.

3 Bake on the lowest shelf in the oven for
15 minutes, then transfer to the middle shelf to bake
for a further 15 minutes, or until top is golden brown.
Allow to cool in the tin. Slice into pieces and serve.

Raspberry cheesecake brownies

MAKES 20 PIECES

250 g (9 oz) milk chocolate, chopped
200 g (7 oz) unsalted butter, softened
185 g (6½ oz/1 cup) soft brown sugar
4 eggs
60 g (2¼ oz/½ cup) self-raising flour, sifted
30 g (1 oz/¼ cup) unsweetened cocoa
powder, sifted
250 g (9 oz/1 cup) cream cheese, at
room temperature
55 g (2 oz/¼ cup) caster (superfine) sugar
125 g (4½ oz/1 cup) frozen raspberries

1 Preheat the oven to 170°C (325°F/Gas 3).
Lightly grease a 16 x 26 cm (6¼ x 10½ inch) baking
tin and line the base with baking paper, extending
the paper over the long sides for easy removal later.

2 Place the chocolate in a heatproof bowl. Half-fill a
saucepan with water, bring to the boil and remove
from the heat. Place the bowl over the saucepan,
ensuring the base of the bowl doesn't touch the
water. Stir occasionally until chocolate has melted.
Cool slightly. »

3 Beat the butter and the brown sugar in a large bowl using electric beaters until thick and creamy. Add three of the eggs, one at a time, beating well after each addition. Fold in the flour and cocoa. Fold in the cooled chocolate and set aside.

4 Clean the electric beaters and beat the cream cheese and caster sugar in a bowl until combined. Add the remaining egg and beat well. Fold in the raspberries.

5 Place alternate layers of the chocolate mixture and cream cheese mixture in the tin. Use a skewer to swirl through mixture to create a marbled effect. Bake for 50 minutes, or until firm. Cool completely in the tin before cutting into squares.

Apple tatin slice with brown sugar cream

MAKES 8 PIECES

3 fuji apples, peeled
60 g (2¼ oz/¼ cup) unsalted butter, chopped
115 g (4 oz/½ cup) caster (superfine) sugar
1 sheet ready-made puff pastry

BROWN SUGAR CREAM
300 ml (10½ fl oz) thick
(double/heavy) cream
2 tablespoons soft brown sugar

1 Preheat the oven to 220°C (425°F/Gas 7).
Lightly grease a 20 cm (8 inch) square baking tin
and line the base and the sides with baking paper,
extending paper over two opposite sides for easy
removal later.

2 Quarter the apples and remove the cores. Cut each
quarter into three wedges.

3 Melt the butter in a saucepan. Add the sugar and
apple and cook, stirring occasionally, for 25 minutes,
or until caramelised. Quickly pour into the prepared
tin and spread with a spatula to cover the base. **»**

4 Trim the puff pastry to 22 cm (8½ inches) square, place over the apple mixture, tucking the edges of the pastry down the inside of the tin and bake for 20–25 minutes, or until the pastry is golden. Allow to stand for 5 minutes before carefully turning the apple tatin out of the tin.

5 To make the brown sugar cream, gently whisk the cream and sugar in a small bowl until combined.

6 Cut the warm apple tatin into pieces and serve immediately with the brown sugar cream.

Hazelnut meringue and chocolate layer slice

MAKES 18 PIECES

100 g (3½ oz/¾ cup) hazelnuts, lightly
toasted and skinned
30 g (1 oz/¼ cup) cornflour (cornstarch)
40 g (1½ oz/⅓ cup) icing (confectioners')
sugar
5 egg whites
200 g (7 oz) caster (superfine) sugar
unsweetened cocoa powder, sifted,
for dusting

GANACHE
250 g (9 oz) dark chocolate, chopped
125 ml (4 fl oz/½ cup) cream
2 tablespoons Frangelico

1 Preheat the oven to 170°C (325°F/Gas 3).
Lightly grease two 26 x 38 cm (10½ x 15 inch)
baking trays and line with baking paper.

2 Place the hazelnuts, cornflour and icing sugar
in the bowl of a food processor and process in
short bursts until the mixture resembles coarse
breadcrumbs. »

3 Beat the egg whites in a large bowl using electric beaters until soft peaks form. Gradually add caster sugar and beat until thick and glossy. Lightly fold the egg whites into the hazelnut mixture.

4 Divide mixture evenly between the two trays and smooth the surface with a spatula. Bake for 30 minutes, or until light golden.

5 Trim edges and cut a 26 cm (10½ inch) square from each meringue, reserving the trimmings. Allow to cool completely.

6 To make ganache, place the chocolate, cream and Frangelico in a heatproof bowl. Half-fill a saucepan with water, bring to the boil and remove from the heat. Sit the bowl over the pan, making sure it does not touch the water. Stir occasionally, until the chocolate has just melted. Leave to cool completely, stirring occasionally.

7 Line a 26 cm (10½ inch) square baking tin with baking paper, extending the paper over two opposite sides. Line the base with one meringue square and carefully spread on half the ganache. Place reserved meringue trimmings side by side over the ganache, then smooth the remaining ganache over the top. Finish with the remaining meringue square, press down gently and refrigerate for 1 hour. Remove the slice from the refrigerator. Dust with cocoa and cut into thin fingers with a serrated knife.

Raspberry and coconut slice

MAKES 12 PIECES

280 g (10 oz/2¼ cups) plain
(all-purpose) flour
3 tablespoons ground almonds
450 g (1 lb/2 cups) caster (superfine) sugar
250 g (9 oz/1 cup) unsalted butter, chilled
and cut into cubes
½ teaspoon ground nutmeg
½ teaspoon baking powder
4 eggs
1 teaspoon natural vanilla extract
1 tablespoon lemon juice
300 g (10½ oz) fresh or thawed
frozen raspberries
90 g (3¼ oz/1 cup) desiccated coconut
icing (confectioners') sugar, sifted,
for dusting

1 Preheat the oven to 180°C (350°F/Gas 4).
Lightly grease a 20 x 30 cm (8 x 12 inch) baking tin
and line the base with baking paper, extending the
paper over two long sides for easy removal later. **»**

2 Sift 220 g (7¾ oz/1¾ cups) of the flour into a large bowl. Add the almonds and 115 g (4 oz/½ cup) of the sugar and stir to combine. Rub in the butter with your fingertips until the mixture resembles fine breadcrumbs. Press into the prepared tin and then bake for 20–25 minutes, or until golden.

3 Reduce the oven temperature to 150°C (300°F/ Gas 2). Sift nutmeg, baking powder and remaining flour onto a piece of baking paper. Beat the eggs, vanilla and remaining caster sugar in a large bowl with electric beaters for 4 minutes, or until light and creamy. Fold in the flour mixture with a large metal spoon. Stir in lemon juice, raspberries and coconut, then pour over the base. Bake for 1 hour, or until golden brown. You may need to cover with foil if the top browns too quickly. Set aside to cool in the tin, then cut into pieces. Dust with the icing sugar and serve.

Choc honeycomb slice

MAKES 18 PIECES

100 g (3½ oz) unsalted butter,
roughly chopped
300 g (10½ oz) milk chocolate,
roughly chopped
115 g (4 oz/⅓ cup) golden syrup
(light treacle)
200 g (7 oz) digestive biscuits (cookies),
roughly broken up
100 g (3½ oz) honeycomb, roughly broken up

1 Lightly grease a 16 x 26 cm (6¼ x 10½ inch) baking tin and line the base and sides with baking paper, extending the paper over the long sides for easy removal later.

2 Place the butter, chocolate and golden syrup in a saucepan. Cook, stirring occasionally, over low heat for 5 minutes, or until the chocolate has melted. Stir through the biscuits and honeycomb. Pour into the prepared tin and use a spatula to smooth the top. Refrigerate until set. Cut into pieces and serve.

Truffle macaroon slice

MAKES 24 PIECES

3 egg whites
170 g (6 oz/¾ cup) caster (superfine) sugar
180 g (6¼ oz/2 cups) desiccated coconut
250 g (9 oz) dark chocolate, chopped
300 ml (10½ fl oz) cream
1 tablespoon unsweetened cocoa powder,
sifted, for dusting

1 Preheat the oven to 180°C (350°F/Gas 4).
Lightly grease a 20 x 30 cm (8 x 12 inch) baking tin
and line the base with baking paper, extending the
paper over two long sides for easy removal later.

2 Beat the egg whites in a large bowl until soft
peaks form. Gradually add the sugar, beating well
after each addition until stiff and glossy. Fold in the
coconut. Spread into the prepared tin and bake for
20 minutes, or until pale golden brown. While still
warm, lightly but firmly press down into the tin with
a spatula. Cool completely. »

3 Place the chocolate in a heatproof bowl. Half-fill a saucepan with water, bring to the boil, then remove from the heat. Place the bowl over the saucepan, making sure the base of the bowl doesn't touch the water. Stand, stirring occasionally, until the chocolate has melted. Cool slightly.

4 Beat the cream until soft peaks form. Gently fold in the melted chocolate until well combined—do not overmix or it will curdle. Spread over the macaroon base and refrigerate for 3 hours, or until set. Remove from the tin, dust with cocoa and cut into fingers.

Rose cheesecake slice

MAKES 15 PIECES

250 g (9 oz) plain sweet biscuits (cookies)
150 g (5½ oz) unsalted butter, melted
100 g (3½ oz) white chocolate, chopped
125 g (4½ oz/½ cup) cream cheese, at
room temperature
2 tablespoons caster (superfine) sugar
90 g (3¼ oz/⅓ cup) sour cream
2 tablespoons boiling water
2 teaspoons powdered gelatine
150 ml (5 fl oz) cream, lightly whipped

ROSE JELLY
220 g (7¾ oz/1 cup) sugar
250 ml (9 fl oz/1 cup) water
400 ml (14 fl oz) pink Champagne
2 drops of rosewater
1½ tablespoons powdered gelatine
15 edible rose petals (optional)

1 Preheat oven to 170°C (325°F/Gas 3). Grease a
16 x 26 cm (6¼ x 10½ inch) baking tin. Line the base
with baking paper, extending paper over the sides.

2 Place the biscuits in the bowl of a food processor.
Process until ground. Add the butter and pulse in
short bursts until combined. Press mixture into tin.
Refrigerate for 20 minutes. Bake for 15 minutes, until
golden. Allow to cool. »

3 Place chocolate in a heatproof bowl. Half-fill a pan with water, bring to the boil and remove from heat. Sit bowl over the pan, ensuring it doesn't touch the water. Stir occasionally, until melted. Cool slightly.

4 Place cream cheese, sugar and sour cream in a bowl and beat with electric beaters until well combined and smooth.

5 Pour the boiling water into a small, heatproof bowl. Add the gelatine and stir until dissolved completely. Stir into the melted chocolate. Fold in the whipped cream and cream cheese mixture, spoon over the base and place in the refrigerator until set.

6 To make the rose jelly, place the sugar and water in a saucepan. Cook, stirring, over low heat until the sugar dissolves. Simmer, without stirring, for 5 minutes, or until reduced and syrupy. Stir in the Champagne and the rosewater, sprinkle over the gelatine and whisk to combine. Pour into a bowl, refrigerate for 2 hours, or until nearly set. Carefully spoon the rose jelly over the filling, smoothing the surface. Refrigerate until set. Cut into squares. Decorate with rose petals.

Double chocolate mud brownies

MAKES 25 PIECES

50 g (9 oz) dark chocolate (54 per cent cocoa solids), chopped
150 g (5½ oz) unsalted butter, cubed
170 g (6 oz/¾ cup) caster (superfine) sugar
3 eggs, at room temperature, lightly whisked
60 g (2¼ oz/½ cup) plain (all-purpose) flour
½ teaspoon baking powder
150 g (5½ oz) milk chocolate, roughly chopped
unsweetened cocoa powder or icing (confectioners') sugar, sifted, for dusting

1 Preheat the oven to 160°C (315°F/Gas 2–3). Grease a 20 cm (8 inch) square cake tin and line base and two opposite sides with baking paper, extending paper over sides for easy removal later.

2 Place the dark chocolate and butter in a heatproof bowl over a saucepan of simmering water, ensuring that the bowl doesn't touch the water. Stir until the chocolate and butter have melted. Remove from the heat and set aside to cool to lukewarm. »

3 Add sugar and eggs to the chocolate mixture and whisk until well combined. Sift in flour and baking powder and whisk until just combined, then, using a wooden spoon, stir in the milk chocolate. Pour into the prepared tin and bake for 45–50 minutes, or until moist crumbs cling to a skewer inserted in the centre. Set aside to cool in the tin.

4 Remove brownie from the tin, using the baking paper. Cut into 4 cm (1½ inch) squares. Dust with the cocoa or icing sugar and serve.

5 These brownies will keep, stored in an airtight container at room temperature, for up to 5 days.

Quince linzer slice

MAKES 16 PIECES

110 g (3¾ oz) plain (all-purpose) flour
110 g (3¾ oz) unsalted butter, chilled and
cut into cubes
55 g (2 oz/¼ cup) caster (superfine) sugar
100 g (3½ oz/1 cup) ground almonds
¼ teaspoon ground cinnamon
1 egg yolk, lightly beaten
2 teaspoons finely grated lemon zest
1 tablespoon lemon juice
200 g (7 oz) quince jam, slightly warmed
icing (confectioners') sugar, sifted, for
dusting (optional)

1 Preheat the oven to 180°C (350°F/Gas 4).
Lightly grease a 20 cm (8 inch) square baking tin
and line base with baking paper, extending paper
over two opposite sides for easy removal later. **»**

2 Sift flour into a large bowl. Rub the butter cubes into the flour with your fingertips until the mixture resembles fine breadcrumbs. Stir in the sugar, the ground almonds and cinnamon. Make a well in the centre and add the egg yolk, lemon zest and juice. Mix with a flat-bladed knife, using a cutting action, until the mixture comes together in beads. Gather together and place on a lightly floured work surface. Shape into a ball, flatten slightly, wrap in plastic wrap and chill in the refrigerator for at least 1 hour.

3 Lightly flour a work surface and roll out two-thirds of the pastry to fit the base of the prepared tin. Press into the tin and refrigerate for 30 minutes. Prick the base all over with a fork, then spread on the jam.

4 Cut remaining dough into strips and arrange over the jam in a lattice pattern. Bake for 35–40 minutes, or until the pastry is golden brown. Set aside to cool slightly, then dust with the icing sugar, if desired, while still warm. Cut into pieces and serve.

BISCUITS

Vanilla sugar hearts

185 g (6½ oz/¾ cup) unsalted
butter, softened
230 g (8½ oz/1 cup) caster (superfine) sugar
2 teaspoons natural vanilla extract
1 egg
310 g (11 oz/2½ cups) plain
(all-purpose) flour
75 g (2⅔ oz/⅓ cup) white sugar

1 Cream butter, sugar and vanilla in a medium-sized bowl using electric beaters until pale and fluffy, then add the egg, beating until just combined. Sift in the flour and stir with a wooden spoon to form a soft dough. Divide the mixture in two, shape the halves into discs, cover with plastic wrap and refrigerate for 1 hour.

2 Preheat the oven to 180°C (350°F/Gas 4). Line two baking trays with baking paper. »

3 Roll the dough out between two pieces of baking paper to 5 mm (¼ inch) thick. Cut the dough into heart shapes using a 5.5 cm (2¼ inch) heart-shaped biscuit cutter, re-rolling the scraps and cutting more hearts. Place on the prepared trays 4 cm (1½ inches) apart, sprinkle with the sugar and gently press it into the dough.

4 Bake for 8–10 minutes, or until lightly golden around the edges. Allow to cool on the trays for a few minutes, then transfer to a wire rack to cool completely. Repeat with the remaining dough.

5 These biscuits will keep, stored in an airtight container, for up to 1 week.

Pecan and coffee sugar biscuits

MAKES 45

40 g (1½ oz/⅓ cup) icing (confectioners')
sugar
1½ tablespoons very finely ground espresso
coffee beans
100 g (3½ oz/1 cup) pecans
55 g (2 oz/¼ cup) caster (superfine) sugar
185 g (6½ oz/¾ cup) unsalted butter,
softened
1 egg yolk
200 g (7 oz/1⅔ cups) plain
(all-purpose) flour
pinch of salt

1 Preheat the oven to 180°C (350°F/Gas 4). Line two baking trays with baking paper.

2 Combine the icing sugar and ground coffee in a bowl and set aside.

3 Place the pecans and 1 tablespoon of the caster sugar in the bowl of a food processor and process until the mixture resembles fine breadcrumbs. »

4 Cream the butter and the remaining caster sugar in a large bowl using electric beaters until pale and fluffy. Add egg yolk and beat until well combined. Stir in the ground pecan mixture, sift in the flour and salt and mix to form a dough.

5 Roll pieces of the dough into 2.5 cm (1 inch) balls, place on prepared trays and flatten slightly. Bake for 10 minutes, or until lightly golden around edges and cooked through. Transfer to a wire rack and, while the biscuits are still hot, sift the sugar and the coffee mixture over the top. Set aside to cool completely.

Honey jumbles

MAKES 24

125 g (4½ oz/½ cup) unsalted butter,
softened
55 g (2 oz/¼ cup) caster (superfine) sugar
45 g (1¾ oz/¼ cup) soft brown sugar
115 g (4 oz/⅓ cup) honey
1 egg yolk
1 teaspoon natural vanilla extract
250 g (9 oz/2 cups) plain (all-purpose) flour
½ teaspoon bicarbonate of soda
(baking soda)
125 g (4½ oz/1 cup) icing
(confectioners') sugar
1–2 tablespoons lemon juice

1 Preheat the oven to 180°C (350°F/Gas 4). Line two
baking trays with baking paper.

2 Cream butter and sugars in a medium-sized bowl
using electric beaters until pale and fluffy, then add
the honey, egg yolk and vanilla, beating until just
combined. Sift in the flour and bicarbonate of soda
and stir with a wooden spoon to form a soft dough. **»**

3 Shape tablespoons of the dough into logs, place on the prepared trays 5 cm (2 inches) apart and flatten slightly. Bake for 10 minutes, or until lightly golden around the edges. Allow to cool on the trays for a few minutes, then transfer to a wire rack and allow to cool completely.

4 To make the icing, place the icing sugar in a medium-sized bowl. Add enough lemon juice to make a smooth and spreadable consistency. Once the snaps are completely cooled, spread the tops with the icing.

5 Honey jumbles will keep, stored in an airtight container, for up to 3 weeks.

Custard dream stars

MAKES 30

185 g (6½ oz/¾ cup) unsalted
butter, softened
40 g (1½ oz/⅓ cup) icing
(confectioners') sugar
1 teaspoon natural vanilla extract
125 g (4½ oz/1 cup) plain (all-purpose) flour
40 g (1½ oz/⅓ cup) custard powder
small sugar decorations

1 Preheat the oven to 180°C (350°F/Gas 4). Line two baking trays with baking paper.

2 Cream the butter, the sugar and the vanilla in a medium-sized bowl using electric beaters until pale and fluffy. Sift in the flour and custard powder and stir with a wooden spoon to form a soft dough, being careful not to over mix.

3 Transfer the mixture to a piping bag fitted with a 1.5 cm (5/ 8 inch) star nozzle. Pipe mixture well apart onto the prepared baking trays to form star shapes, about 4 cm (1½ inches) in diameter. Place a sugar decoration in the centre of each star. Refrigerate for 20 minutes. »

4 Bake for 12–15 minutes, or until lightly golden, taking care not to burn. Allow to cool on the trays for a few minutes, then transfer to a wire rack to cool completely.

5 Custard dream stars will keep, stored in an airtight container, for up to 5 days.

TIP: You can buy small sugar decorations from most delicatessens and supermarkets.

Lime and sour cream biscuits

MAKES 30

125 g (4½ oz/½ cup) unsalted
butter, softened
230 g (8¼ oz/1 cup) caster (superfine) sugar
1 teaspoon natural vanilla extract
1½ tablespoons finely grated lime zest
90 g (3¼ oz/⅓ cup) sour cream
250 g (9 oz/2 cups) plain (all-purpose) flour
½ teaspoon baking powder

1 Preheat the oven to 180°C (350°F/Gas 4). Line two baking trays with baking paper.

2 Cream butter, sugar and vanilla in a medium-sized bowl using electric beaters until pale and fluffy, then add the lime zest and sour cream, beating until just combined. Sift in the flour and baking powder and stir with a wooden spoon to form a soft dough. **»**

3 Shape tablespoons of the mixture into balls, place on prepared trays 5 cm (2 inches) apart and flatten slightly. Bake for 15 minutes, or until lightly golden around the edges. Allow to cool on the trays for a few minutes, then transfer to a wire rack to cool completely. Repeat with the remaining dough.

4 These biscuits will keep, stored in an airtight container, for up to 1 week.

Classic shortbread

MAKES 16 WEDGES

**225 g (8 oz) unsalted butter, softened
115 g (4 oz/½ cup) caster (superfine) sugar,
plus extra for dusting
210 g (7½ oz/1¾ cups) plain
(all-purpose) flour
115 g (4 oz/⅔ cup) rice flour**

1 Lightly grease two baking trays.
Cream butter and sugar in a medium-sized bowl
using electric beaters until pale and fluffy. Sift in the
flours and a pinch of salt and stir with a wooden
spoon until it resembles fine breadcrumbs. Transfer
to a lightly floured work surface and knead gently to
form a soft dough. Cover with plastic wrap and
refrigerate for 30 minutes.

2 Preheat the oven to 160°C (315°F/Gas 2-3).
Divide the dough in half and roll out one half on a
lightly floured work surface to form a 20 cm (8 inch)
round. Carefully transfer to one of the prepared trays.
Using a sharp knife, score the surface of dough into
eight equal wedges, prick the surface lightly with a
fork and, using your fingers, press the edge to form a
fluted effect. Repeat using the remaining dough to
make a second round. Lightly dust the shortbreads
with the extra sugar. **»**

3 Bake for 35 minutes, or until the shortbreads are pale golden and cooked through. Remove from the oven and while still hot, follow the score marks and cut into wedges. Cool on the baking trays for 5 minutes, then transfer to a wire rack.

4 These shortbread will keep, stored in an airtight container, for up to 1 week.

TIP While shortbread can be made with plain flour alone, adding rice flour produces a lighter result.

Amore biscuits

MAKES 20

250 g (9 oz/2 cups) plain (all-purpose) flour
1 teaspoon baking powder
¼ teaspoon ground mixed spice
60 g (2¼ oz/⅓ cup) soft brown sugar
½ teaspoon finely grated lemon zest
1 egg
1 tablespoon milk
1 teaspoon natural vanilla extract
100 g (3½ oz) unsalted butter, softened
2 teaspoons unsweetened cocoa powder
1 teaspoon brandy
icing (confectioners') sugar, to dust

1 Preheat the oven to 170°C (325°F/Gas 3). Line two baking trays with baking paper.

2 Sift flour, ¼ teaspoon salt, baking powder and mixed spice into a bowl. Add sugar, lemon zest, egg, milk, vanilla and butter and, using electric beaters, mix into a smooth dough. Turn out onto a lightly floured surface and then roll into a smooth ball. Cover with plastic wrap and refrigerate for 20 minutes. »

3 Divide dough in half. On a lightly floured surface, roll out one portion to 3 mm (1/ 8 inch) thick. Cut the dough into ten hearts using a 7 cm (2¾ inch) heart-shaped biscuit cutter. Re-roll out the scraps and cut out ten 1 cm (½ inch) hearts. Place on the prepared trays. Working with the other portion, knead in the cocoa and brandy until just combined, then repeat as above.

4 Lay a small heart onto a large heart of the opposite colour. Bake for 12 minutes, or until lightly golden. Allow to cool on the trays for a few minutes, then transfer to a wire rack to cool completely. Sift over the icing sugar.

5 These will keep, stored in an airtight container, for up to 5 days.

Pecan praline biscuits

MAKES 24

115 g (4 oz/½ cup) caster (superfine) sugar
125 g (4½ oz/½ cup) unsalted
butter, softened
170 g (6 oz/¾ cup) caster (superfine)
sugar, extra
1 teaspoon natural vanilla extract
1 egg yolk
250 g (9 oz/2 cups) plain (all-purpose) flour
1 teaspoon baking powder
150 g (5½ oz/1½ cups) whole pecans

1 Preheat oven to 160°C (350°F/Gas 2–3). Line two baking trays with baking paper.

2 To make the praline, combine caster sugar and 1 tablespoon water in a small saucepan, stirring over low heat until sugar is dissolved. Use a pastry brush to brush down any excess sugar on the side of the saucepan. Once the sugar is dissolved, stop stirring and continue cooking until liquid becomes a golden caramel colour. Pour this toffee onto one of the prepared trays, spreading it out evenly. Allow to cool and harden, then break into pieces. Process in a food processor until finely chopped. Re-line baking tray with baking paper. **»**

3 Cream the butter, extra sugar and vanilla in a medium-sized bowl using electric beaters until pale and fluffy, then add the egg yolk, beating until just combined. Add finely chopped praline and stir to combine. Sift in the flour and baking powder and stir with a wooden spoon to form a soft dough.

4 Shape tablespoons of the dough into small logs and press a pecan into the centre of each. Place on the prepared trays 4 cm (1½ inches) apart and bake for 12–15 minutes, or until lightly golden around the edges. Allow to cool on the trays for a few minutes, then transfer to a wire rack to cool completely.

5 These biscuits will keep, stored in an airtight container, for up to 2 weeks.

Apricot biscuits with lemon icing

160 g (5⅔ oz/⅔ cup) unsalted
butter, softened
170 g (6 oz/¾ cup) caster (superfine) sugar
2 tablespoons marmalade
1 teaspoon natural vanilla extract
200 g (7 oz) dried apricots, chopped
125 g (4½ oz/1 cup) self-raising flour
40 g (1½ oz/⅓ cup) plain (all-purpose) flour
125 g (4½ oz/1 cup) icing (confectioners')
sugar
2 teaspoons lemon juice

1 Line two baking trays with baking paper.
Cream the butter and the sugar in a medium-sized
bowl using electric beaters until light and creamy.
Add the marmalade, the vanilla and apricots and
mix until well combined.

2 Sift flours into a large bowl and then stir in butter
mixture. Turn out onto a lightly floured surface and
bring together until just smooth. Divide in half. Place
each portion on a sheet of baking paper and roll up
in the paper to form two logs, 21 cm (8¼ inches) long
and 4.5 cm (1¾ inches) thick. Lay on a tray and place
in the refrigerator for 15 minutes until firm. **»**

3 Preheat the oven to 180°C (350°F/Gas 4). Remove the baking paper and, using a serrated knife, cut logs into 1 cm (½ inch) diagonal slices. Place well apart on the prepared trays. Bake for 10–15 minutes, or until golden. Allow to cool on the trays for at least 5 minutes, then transfer to a wire rack to cool completely. Repeat with the remaining dough.

4 To make the icing, sift the icing sugar into a small bowl. Add the lemon juice and 3 teaspoons hot water and stir until smooth. Place in a small paper or plastic piping bag. Seal the end and snip off the tip. Decorate the biscuits with the icing.

5 These biscuits will keep, stored in an airtight container, for up to 5 days.

Cardamom crescents

MAKES 30

60 g (2¼ oz/½ cup) slivered almonds
250 g (9 oz/1 cup) unsalted butter, softened
3 tablespoons icing (confectioners')
sugar, sifted
2 tablespoons brandy
1 teaspoon finely grated lime zest
310 g (11 oz/2½ cups) plain
(all-purpose) flour
1 teaspoon ground cardamom
icing (confectioners') sugar, extra, to dust
and to store (optional)

1 Preheat the oven to 180°C (350°F/Gas 4). Line two baking trays with baking paper. Put the almonds on another baking tray and bake for 5 minutes, or until lightly golden. Allow to cool and finely chop.

2 Cream butter and sugar in a medium-sized bowl using electric beaters until pale and fluffy, then mix in the brandy, lime zest and the toasted almonds. Sift in flour and cardamom and stir with a wooden spoon to form a soft dough. »

3 Shape tablespoons of dough into small crescents and place on the prepared trays well apart. Bake for 15–20 minutes, or until lightly golden. Allow to cool on the trays for a few minutes, then transfer to a wire rack to cool completely.

4 To serve, sift over some of the icing sugar to cover the crescents completely. If storing the crescents, place in a tin or plastic box and cover entirely with the remaining icing sugar.

5 The crescents will keep, stored in an airtight container, for up to 5 days.

Almond and coffee meringue hearts

MAKES 40

3 egg whites
335 g (11¾ oz/2⅔ cups) icing
(confectioners') sugar, sifted, plus extra
for dusting
½ teaspoon lemon juice
finely grated zest of ½ lemon
200 g (7 oz/2 cups) ground almonds
1 teaspoon ground cinnamon
2 teaspoons finely ground espresso
coffee beans

1 Place egg whites in a large bowl and beat using electric beaters until stiff peaks form. Gradually add the sugar, a spoonful at a time, and beat until sugar has dissolved and the meringue mixture is thick and glossy. Whisk in lemon juice. Remove 150 g (5½ oz/ 1 cup) of the meringue mixture and set aside.

2 Combine lemon zest, ground almonds, cinnamon and coffee in a separate bowl and fold into meringue mixture to form a thick dough. Refrigerate for 1 hour, or until the dough is firm. »

3 Preheat the oven to 180°C (350°F/Gas 4). Line two baking trays with baking paper.

4 Dust a clean work surface with the extra sugar and roll out the dough to 8 mm (3/8 inch) thick. Cut the dough into hearts using a lightly greased 5 cm (2 inch) heart-shaped biscuit cutter and then transfer to the prepared trays. Place teaspoonfuls of the reserved meringue mixture on top of each biscuit shape and spread out evenly using the back of a spoon or a spatula. Set aside for 15 minutes to dry out the meringue. Bake for 10–12 minutes, or until light golden brown around edges. Transfer to a wire rack to cool completely.

Cinnamon circles

50 g (1¾ oz) unsalted butter, softened
80 g (2¾ oz/⅓ cup) caster (superfine) sugar
½ teaspoon natural vanilla extract
85 g (3 oz/⅔ cup) plain (all-purpose) flour
1 tablespoon milk
2 tablespoons caster (superfine)
sugar, extra
½ teaspoon ground cinnamon

1 Preheat the oven to 180°C (350°F/Gas 4). Line two baking trays with baking paper.

2 Cream butter and sugar in a medium-sized bowl using electric beaters until pale and fluffy, then stir in the vanilla. Sift in the flour and add the milk. Stir with a wooden spoon to form a soft dough, gather into a ball and place on a sheet of baking paper.

3 Press dough out to a log shape, 25 cm (10 inches) long and 3 cm (1¼ inches) thick. Roll in the paper and twist ends to seal. Refrigerate for 20 minutes, or until firm. **»**

4 Cut the log into rounds 1 cm (½ inch) thick. Sift extra caster sugar and cinnamon onto a plate and roll each biscuit in the sugar mixture, coating well. Lay well apart on the prepared trays and bake for 20 minutes, or until lightly golden around the edges. Allow to cool on the trays for a few minutes, then transfer to a wire rack to cool completely.

5 These biscuits will keep, stored in an airtight container, for up to 5 days.

Orange polenta biscuits

MAKES 20–22

125 g (4½ oz/½ cup) unsalted
butter, softened
80 g (2¾ oz/⅓ cup) caster (superfine) sugar
1 teaspoon orange flower water
finely grated zest from 1 orange
2 eggs
165 g (5¾ oz/1⅓ cups) plain
(all-purpose) flour
80 g (2¾ oz/½ cup) polenta

1 Preheat the oven to 200°C (400°F/Gas 6). Line two baking trays with baking paper.

2 Combine butter, sugar, orange flower water and orange zest in a food processor and process until light and creamy. Add the eggs and process until smooth. Add the flour and the polenta and pulse until a sticky dough forms.

3 Transfer mixture to a piping bag fitted with a 2 cm (¾ inch) star nozzle. Pipe mixture onto the prepared baking trays to form 7 cm (2¾ inch) crescents. Bake for 15 minutes, or until the lightly golden around the edges. Cool on trays for a few minutes, then transfer to a wire rack to cool completely.

4 Orange polenta biscuits will keep, stored in an airtight container, for up to 3 days.

Lemon curd sandwiches

MAKES 24

110 g (3¾ oz) unsalted butter, softened
115 g (4 oz/½ cup) caster (superfine) sugar
½ teaspoon natural vanilla extract
2 teaspoons finely grated lemon zest
1 egg yolk
155 g (5½ oz/1¼ cups) plain
(all-purpose) flour
30 g (1 oz/¼ cup) icing (confectioners')
sugar, for dusting

LEMON CURD
juice from 2 lemons
80 g (2¾ oz/⅓ cup) caster (superfine) sugar
3 teaspoons cornflour (cornstarch)
4 egg yolks
finely grated zest from 1 lemon »

1 To make the lemon curd, combine lemon juice, sugar and the cornflour in a small saucepan and, over low heat, whisk until combined. Slowly bring to the boil, stirring with a wooden spoon until the mixture thickens. Remove from heat and whisk in the egg yolks and zest. Return to a gentle heat and cook for 2–3 minutes, stirring until well combined and thickened. Remove from the heat and place the curd in a heatproof bowl. Place plastic wrap on the surface of the curd to stop a skin forming and set aside to cool. This can be made in advance, and needs to be refrigerated.

2 Preheat the oven to 170°C (325°F/Gas 3). Line two baking trays with baking paper.

3 Cream butter, sugar and vanilla in a bowl using electric beaters until pale and fluffy, then add lemon zest and egg yolk, beating until just combined. Sift in the flour and, using a wooden spoon, stir until it forms a soft dough. Turn out the dough, and gently shape it into a flat disc. Cover with plastic wrap and refrigerate for 20 minutes.Roll dough out between two pieces of baking paper to 3 mm (⅛ inch) thick. Cut dough into round and ring shapes, alternating between 4.5 cm (1¾ inch) round-shaped cutter and a 4.5 cm (1¾ inch) ring-shaped cutter so you end up with the same amount of each shape. Re-roll any leftover dough scraps and then cut more rounds and rings. **»**

4 Place on the prepared trays 3 cm (1¼ inches) apart and bake for 9 minutes, or until lightly golden around the edges. Cool on the trays for a few minutes, then transfer to a wire rack to allow to cool completely. Repeat with the remaining dough.

5 On the biscuit rounds, place a teaspoon of the lemon curd, flatten a little with a knife and then sandwich it together with a ring biscuit, pressing down on the curd so it goes right to the edge. Dust the biscuits with the icing sugar. Repeat with the remaining biscuits.

6 Filled biscuits will keep, stored in an airtight container for 3 days. Unfilled biscuits will keep, stored in an airtight container, for up to 3 weeks.

Molasses moons

MAKES 60

125 g (4½ oz/½ cup) unsalted butter,
softened
185 g (6½ oz/1 cup) soft brown sugar
2 tablespoons molasses
1 egg yolk
250 g (9 oz/2 cups) plain (all-purpose) flour
½ teaspoon bicarbonate of soda
(baking soda)
1 teaspoon ground mixed spice

1 Cream the butter and sugar in a medium-sized
bowl using electric beaters until pale and fluffy, then
add the molasses and egg yolk, beating until just
combined. Sift in the flour, bicarbonate of soda and
mixed spice and stir with a wooden spoon to form a
soft dough. Cover with plastic wrap and refrigerate
for 2 hours.

2 Preheat the oven to 160°C (315°F/Gas 2–3).
Line two baking trays with baking paper. **»**

3 Divide the dough in two portions and roll each between two pieces of baking paper to 5 mm (¼ inch) thick. Cut dough into moon shapes using a 6 cm (2½ inch) moon-shaped cutter, re-rolling the scraps and cutting more moons. Place on prepared trays 5 cm (2 inches) apart and bake for 7 minutes. Allow to cool on the trays for a few minutes, then transfer to a wire rack to cool completely. Repeat with the remaining dough.

4 Molasses moons will keep, stored in an airtight container, for up to 3 weeks.

Ginger fingers

MAKES 25

100 g (3½ oz/¾ cup) chopped
macadamia nuts
250 g (9 oz/1 cup) unsalted butter, softened
80 g (2¾ oz/⅓ cup) caster (superfine) sugar
100 g (3½ oz) glacé ginger, chopped
250 g (9 oz/2 cups) plain (all-purpose) flour
90 g (3¼ oz/½ cup) rice flour
caster (superfine) sugar, to sprinkle

1 Preheat oven to 150°C (300°F/Gas 2). Line a large
baking tray with baking paper. Lay macadamias on
another baking tray and toast for 3–5 minutes, or
until lightly golden. Set aside to cool.

2 Cream butter and sugar in a medium-sized bowl
using electric beaters until pale and fluffy. Mix in the
ginger and nuts. Sift in flours and stir with a wooden
spoon to form a dough. **»**

3 Gather the dough into a ball and roll out to a 1 cm (½ inch) thick rectangle. Cut the rectangle into 3 x 7 cm (1¼ x 2¾ inch) fingers. Place on the prepared tray and sprinkle with the caster sugar. Bake for 35 minutes, or until the ginger fingers are pale golden underneath. Allow to cool on the tray for a few minutes, then transfer to a wire rack to cool completely.

4 Ginger fingers will keep, stored in an airtight container, for up to 2 days.

Chocolate mud biscuits

MAKES 36

250 g (9 oz/1²⁄₃ cups) chopped
dark chocolate
125 g (4½ oz/½ cup) unsalted
butter, softened
185 g (6½ oz/1 cup) soft brown sugar
1 teaspoon natural vanilla extract
1 egg
185 g (6½ oz/1½ cups) plain
(all-purpose) flour
40 g (1½ oz/⅓ cup) unsweetened
cocoa powder

1 Preheat the oven to 180°C (350°F/Gas 4). Line two baking trays with baking paper.

2 Place the chocolate in a food processor and pulse until finely chopped, then set aside. **»**

3 Cream the butter, sugar and vanilla in a medium bowl using electric beaters until pale and fluffy, then add the egg, beating until just combined. Sift in the flour and cocoa, add the chopped chocolate and stir with a wooden spoon to form a soft dough.

4 Shape tablespoons of the dough into balls, place on the prepared trays well apart from each other and flatten into 4.5 cm (1¾ inch) rounds. Bake for 9 minutes. Cool on the trays for a few minutes, then transfer to a wire rack to cool completely.

5 These biscuits will keep, stored in an airtight container, for up to 1 week.

Chocolate shortbread

MAKES 65

150 g (5½ oz/1 cup) chopped dark chocolate
250 g (9 oz/1 cup) unsalted butter, softened
115 g (4 oz/½ cup) caster (superfine) sugar
310 g (11 oz/2½ cups) plain
(all-purpose) flour
2 tablespoons unsweetened cocoa powder
1 tablespoon drinking chocolate

1 Preheat the oven to 160°C (315°F/Gas 2–3).
Lightly grease two baking trays.

2 Place the chocolate in a heatproof bowl over a
saucepan of simmering water, ensuring the bowl
doesn't touch the water. Stir until the chocolate has
melted. Set aside to cool for 5 minutes.

3 Cream butter and sugar in a medium-sized bowl
using electric beaters until pale and fluffy, then add
the melted chocolate. Sift in the flour and stir with a
wooden spoon to form a soft dough. **»**

4 Shape tablespoons of the dough into balls, place on the prepared trays well apart and flatten slightly. Bake for 12–15 minutes. Allow to cool on the trays for a few minutes, then transfer to a wire rack to cool completely. Repeat with the remaining dough.

5 Just before serving, sift the combined cocoa and drinking chocolate over the shortbread to dust.

6 These shortbread will keep, stored in an airtight container, for up to 1 week.

Walnut and orange biscotti

MAKES 40

310 g (11 oz/2½ cups) plain (all-purpose)
flour, plus extra for rolling
1 teaspoon baking powder
½ teaspoon bicarbonate of soda
(baking soda)
170 g (6 oz/¾ cup) caster (superfine) sugar
3 eggs, lightly beaten
finely grated zest from 3 oranges
2 teaspoons natural vanilla extract
250 g (9 oz/2½ cups) walnut halves, lightly
toasted and roughly chopped

1 Preheat the oven to 170°C (325°F/Gas 3).
Lightly grease a large baking tray.

2 Sift flour, baking powder and bicarbonate of soda
into a large bowl, then stir in the sugar. Combine the
eggs, orange zest and vanilla in a bowl and stir with
a fork to mix well. Pour the egg mixture into the flour
mixture and stir until nearly combined, then, using
your hands, knead briefly to form a firm dough. Put
dough on a lightly floured work surface and knead
the walnuts into the dough. »

3 Divide the dough into three even-sized pieces. Working with one piece of dough at a time, roll to form a 29 cm (11½ inch) log. Gently pat the surface to flatten the log to a 4 cm (1½ inch) width, then place the logs on the prepared tray and bake for 30 minutes, or until they are light golden and firm. Remove from oven and allow to cool for 15 minutes.

4 Reduce oven temperature to 150°C (300°F/Gas 2). When the logs are cool enough to handle, cut them on the diagonal into 1 cm (½ inch) thick slices. Arrange them in a single layer on two baking trays and bake for 15 minutes, or until the biscotti are dry, swapping the position of the trays halfway through cooking. Allow to cool on a wire rack.

5 Biscotti will keep, stored in an airtight container, for up to 3 weeks.

Lime and coconut shortbreads

MAKES 25

250 g (9 oz/2 cups) plain (all-purpose) flour
40 g (1½ oz/⅓ cup) icing
(confectioners') sugar
65 g (2¼ oz/¾ cup) desiccated coconut
2 teaspoons finely grated lime zest
200 g (7 oz) unsalted butter, cubed
and chilled
1 tablespoon lime juice

ICING
125 g (4½ oz/1 cup) icing (confectioners')
sugar, extra
2 tablespoons lime juice, extra, strained

1 Preheat the oven to 180°C (350°F/Gas 4). Line two baking trays with baking paper.

2 Sift flour and icing sugar into a bowl and stir in the coconut and lime zest. Add butter and rub in with your fingertips until crumbly. Add the lime juice and cut into the flour mixture using a flat-bladed knife. »

3 Gather the dough into a ball and roll out on a lightly floured work surface to 5 mm (¼ inch) thick. Using a 5 cm (2 inch) biscuit cutter, cut into rounds. Lay well apart on the prepared trays and bake for 15–20 minutes, or until very lightly golden. Allow to cool on the trays for a few minutes, then transfer to a wire rack to cool completely.

4 To make icing, sift the extra icing sugar into a small heatproof bowl, add the extra lime juice and place over a saucepan of simmering water. Stir until smooth. Spoon a little icing onto each shortbread, stirring the icing in the bowl occasionally to prevent it from hardening, and spread evenly. Leave the shortbread on the wire rack to set.

5 These shortbread will keep, stored in an airtight container, for up to 5 days.

Coffee wafers

MAKES 60

185 g (6½ oz/¾ cup) unsalted
butter, softened
170 g (6 oz/¾ cup) caster (superfine) sugar
45 g (1¾ oz/¼ cup) dark brown sugar
1 teaspoon natural vanilla extract
1 egg yolk
1 tablespoon milk
60 ml (2 fl oz/¼ cup) strong espresso coffee
375 g (13 oz/3 cups) plain (all-purpose) flour

COFFEE ICING
125 g (4½ oz/1 cup) icing (confectioners')
sugar, sifted
1 tablespoon espresso coffee
coffee beans, to decorate

1 Preheat the oven to 180°C (350°F/Gas 4). Line two
baking trays with baking paper.

2 Cream the butter and sugars in a large bowl using
electric beaters until pale and fluffy, then add the
vanilla, egg yolk, milk and coffee, beating until just
combined. Sift in the flour and stir with a wooden
spoon to form a soft dough. »

3 Turn the dough out onto a lightly floured work surface and knead gently until the mixture comes together. Divide mixture into two and roll each portion between two pieces of baking paper to 5 mm (¼ inch). Cut the dough into rounds using a 5 cm (2 inch) round biscuit cutter, re-rolling dough scraps and cutting out more rounds. Place on the prepared trays 3 cm (1¼ inches) apart and bake for 10 minutes, or until golden around the edges. Allow to cool on the trays for a few minutes, then transfer to a wire rack to cool completely. Repeat with the remaining dough.

4 To make the coffee icing, place the icing sugar and coffee in a small bowl and stir until smooth. Using a spoon, spread a circle of icing on top of each wafer and top with coffee beans.

5 These wafers will keep, stored in an airtight container, for up to 2 weeks.

Cinnamon chocolate kisses

MAKES ABOUT 50

250 g (9 oz/1 cup) unsalted butter, softened
85 g (3 oz/⅔ cup) icing (confectioners') sugar
155 g (5½ oz/1¼ cups) plain
(all-purpose) flour
40 g (1½ oz/⅓ cup) cornflour (cornstarch)
30 g (1 oz/¼ cup) unsweetened
cocoa powder
2½ teaspoons ground cinnamon

CHOCOLATE GANACHE
80 ml (2½ fl oz/⅓ cup) cream (whipping)
120 g (4¼ oz) dark chocolate (54 per cent
cocoa solids), finely chopped

1 Preheat the oven to 160°C (315°F/Gas 2–3).
Line two baking trays with baking paper. »

2 Cream the butter and sugar in a medium-sized bowl using electric beaters until pale and fluffy. Sift in the flour, cornflour, cocoa and cinnamon and beat until just combined. Spoon the mixture into a piping (icing) bag fitted with a 1 cm (½ inch) star nozzle. Pipe 3 cm (1¼ inch) stars, about 2 cm (¾ inch) apart, onto the prepared trays. Place in the refrigerator for 20 minutes. Bake, swapping trays halfway through cooking, for 20 minutes, or until just cooked through. Allow the biscuits to cool on the trays.

3 Meanwhile, to make chocolate ganache, heat the cream in a small saucepan until almost simmering. Place the chocolate in a heatproof bowl and pour on the hot cream. Stand for 1 minute, then stir until the chocolate has melted. Cover with plastic wrap and place in the refrigerator, stirring occasionally, for 30 minutes, or until the ganache becomes a thick, spreadable consistency.

4 Spread the base of half the biscuits with chocolate ganache and then sandwich together with the rest of the biscuits.

5 These kisses will keep, stored in an airtight container, for up to 5 days.

TIP These cinnamon chocolate kisses are also delicious unfilled and dusted with icing (confectioners') sugar.

Fruit almond bread

3 egg whites
125 g (4½ oz) caster (superfine) sugar
125 g (4½ oz/1 cup) plain (all-purpose)
flour, sifted
125 g (4½ oz) whole almonds
100 g (3½ oz/½ cup) glacé cherries
30 g (1 oz) glacé apricots, cut into pieces the
same size as the cherries
30 g (1 oz) glacé pineapple, cut into pieces
the same size as the almonds

1 Preheat the oven to 180°C (350°F/Gas 4). Lightly grease a 25 x 8 cm (10 x 3¼ inch) loaf (bar) tin and line it with baking paper.

2 Whisk egg whites in a bowl until soft peaks form, then gradually add the sugar, whisking continuously. Continue whisking until very stiff peaks form, and then fold through the flour. Gently fold in almonds and the glacé fruits. Transfer mixture to the prepared tin, smooth the surface and bake for 30–40 minutes, or until firm to the touch. **»**

3 Cool in the tin for 10 minutes, then turn out and peel off the baking paper. Cool completely on a wire rack, then wrap in foil and set aside for 1–2 days.

4 Preheat the oven to 140°C (275°F/Gas 1) and line a baking tray with baking paper. Using a very sharp knife, cut the loaf into wafer-thin slices. Spread onto the baking tray and bake for 45–50 minutes, until dry and crisp. Allow to cool on trays for a few minutes, then transfer to a wire rack to cool completely.

5 Almond fruit bread will keep, stored in an airtight container, for up to 5 days.

Strawberry pecan biscuits

MAKES 32

160 g (5⅔ oz/⅔ cup) unsalted
butter, softened
170 g (6 oz/¾ cup) caster (superfine) sugar
½ teaspoon natural vanilla extract
80 g (2¾ oz/⅓ cup) fresh strawberry purée
100 g (3½ oz/½ cup) dried strawberries,
thinly sliced
80 g (2¾ oz) ground pecans
185 g (6½ oz/1½ cups) plain
(all-purpose) flour
300 g (10½ oz) white chocolate, chopped
red food colouring

1 Preheat the oven to 180°C (350°F/Gas 4). Line two baking trays with baking paper.

2 Cream the butter, sugar and vanilla in a bowl using electric beaters until pale and fluffy. Mix in the strawberry purée, the dried strawberries and the ground pecans. Sift in the flour and stir until it forms a soft dough. **»**

3 Shape tablespoons of the dough into balls and put on the prepared trays 5 cm (2 inches) apart. Flatten slightly and bake for 12–15 minutes, or until lightly golden around the edges. Allow to cool on the trays for a few minutes, then transfer to a wire rack to cool completely. Repeat with the remaining dough.

4 Place the chocolate in a heatproof bowl over a saucepan of simmering water, ensuring the bowl doesn't touch the water. Stir until chocolate has melted. Remove from the heat and stir in the food colouring, a drop at a time, until chocolate is pale pink. Dip each biscuit into the chocolate to coat half of it. Place on a lined baking tray for about 40 minutes to set.

5 These biscuits will keep, stored in an airtight container, for up to 1 week.

Sesame and ginger wafers

MAKES 36

40 g (1½ oz) unsalted butter
40 g (1½ oz) caster (superfine) sugar
2 tablespoons golden syrup (light treacle)
or dark corn syrup
40 g (1½ oz/⅓ cup) plain (all-purpose) flour
½ teaspoon ground ginger
1 tablespoon brandy
2 teaspoons lemon juice
1 tablespoon sesame seeds, toasted

1 Preheat oven to 190°C (375°F/Gas 5). Grease two baking trays.

2 Combine the butter, sugar and syrup in a small saucepan and heat gently, stirring occasionally, until the butter melts and the mixture is smooth. Remove from the heat.

3 Sift the flour and ginger into a bowl. Add the melted butter mixture and the brandy, lemon juice and sesame seeds and stir to mix well. »

4 Drop ½ teaspoons of the mixture onto the prepared trays (only cook four wafers per tray), leaving enough room to allow for spreading. Use a spatula to spread each wafer out to form a 5 cm (2 inch) round. Bake for 3–4 minutes, or until the wafers begin to brown around the edges. Cool for 1 minute. Using a palette knife and working quickly, carefully remove the warm biscuits from the trays, then quickly drape them over the handle of a wooden spoon to make them curl. Cool completely, then remove from the wooden spoon. Repeat with the remaining mixture.

5 Sesame and ginger wafers are best eaten on the day they are made.

Ginger nut biscuits

MAKES 24

125 g (4½ oz/½ cup) unsalted butter,
softened
185 g (6½ oz/1 cup) soft brown sugar
2 tablespoons golden syrup
1 egg yolk
250 g (9 oz/2 cups) plain (all-purpose) flour
½ teaspoon bicarbonate of soda
(baking soda)
2 teaspoons ground ginger
1 teaspoon ground mixed spice

1 Preheat the oven to 170°C (325°F/Gas 3). Line two baking trays with baking paper.

2 Cream butter and sugar in a medium-sized bowl using electric beaters until pale and fluffy, then add the golden syrup and the egg yolk, beating until just combined. Sift in flour, bicarbonate of soda, ginger and mixed spice and stir with a wooden spoon until a soft dough forms. »

3 Shape tablespoons of the dough into balls, place on the prepared trays about 5 cm (2 inches) apart and flatten into 4 cm (1½ inch) rounds. Bake for 15 minutes, or until lightly golden around the edges. Cool on the trays for a few minutes, then transfer to a wire rack to cool completely.

4 These biscuits will keep, stored in an airtight container, for up to 3 weeks.

Gingerbread biscuits

MAKES 40 (DEPENDING ON SIZE OF CUTTERS)

350 g (12 oz) plain (all-purpose) flour
2 teaspoons baking powder
2 teaspoons ground ginger
100 g (3½ oz) unsalted butter, chilled
and diced
140 g (5 oz/¾ cup) soft brown sugar
1 egg, beaten
115 g (4 oz/⅓ cup) dark treacle
silver balls (optional)

ICING GLAZE
1 egg white
3 teaspoons lemon juice
155 g (5½ oz/1¼ cups) icing
(confectioners') sugar

ROYAL ICING
1 egg white
200 g (7 oz) icing (confectioners') sugar »

1 Preheat the oven to 190°C (375°F/Gas 5). Lightly grease two baking trays.

2 Sift the flour, baking powder, ground ginger and a pinch of salt into a bowl. Rub in the butter with your fingertips until mixture resembles fine breadcrumbs, then stir in the sugar. Make a well in the centre, add the egg and treacle and, using a wooden spoon, stir until a soft dough forms. Transfer to a clean surface and knead until smooth.

3 Divide the dough in half and roll out on a lightly floured work surface until 5 mm (¼ inch) thick. Using various-shaped biscuit cutters (such as hearts and flowers), cut the dough and then transfer to the prepared trays. Bake in batches for 8 minutes, or until the gingerbread is light brown. Allow to cool on trays for a few minutes, then transfer to a wire rack to cool completely. If you would like to use the gingerbread biscuits as hanging decorations, use a skewer to make a hole in each while still hot after baking.

4 To make the icing glaze, whisk the egg white and lemon juice together until foamy, then whisk in the icing sugar to form a smooth, thin icing. Cover the surface with plastic wrap until needed.

5 To make the royal icing, lightly whisk egg white until just foamy, then gradually whisk in enough icing sugar to form a soft icing. Cover the surface with plastic wrap until it is needed. »

6 Brush a thin layer of glaze over some of the gingerbread and leave to set. Use a palette knife to spread the royal icing over the biscuits in a thin layer. Alternatively, fill an icing bag with the royal icing and decorate biscuits as desired.

7 Gingerbread will keep, stored in an airtight container, for up to 3 days.

TIPS To make a paper icing bag, cut a piece of baking paper into a 19 cm (7½ inch) square and then cut in half diagonally to form two triangles. Hold the triangle, with the longest side away from you, and curl the left hand point over and in towards the centre. Repeat with right hand point, forming a cone shape, with both ends meeting neatly in the middle. Staple together at the wide end.

CHOCOLATE
INDULGENCES

Chocolate pecan and golden syrup tarts

MAKES 6

CHOCOLATE PASTRY
185 g (6½ oz/1½ cups) plain (all-purpose)
flour, sifted
2 tablespoons unsweetened cocoa
powder, sifted
2 tablespoons icing (confectioners')
sugar, sifted
150 g (5½ oz) unsalted butter, chilled
and cubed
2 tablespoons chilled water

FILLING
75 g (2¾ oz) dark chocolate (54 per cent
cocoa solids), chopped
75 g (2¾ oz) unsalted butter, cubed
1 egg, at room temperature
1 egg yolk, at room temperature
2 tablespoons golden syrup (light treacle)
1½ tablespoons caster (superfine) sugar
50 g (1¾ oz/½ cup) pecans, lightly toasted
and chopped »

5 This chocolate bark will keep, stored in an airtight container in a cool spot, for up to 2 weeks.

TIPS Dried cherries are available from selected health food and gourmet food stores. You can replace the dried cherries with sweetened dried cranberries, if you wish. Toast the almonds in a preheated 180°C (350°F/Gas 4) oven for 5 minutes, or until lightly golden and aromatic. Allow to cool on the tray.

Chocolate oranges

MAKES 40

**2 medium valencia oranges, ends trimmed,
cut into 5 mm (¼ inch) thick slices
100 g (3½ oz) dark chocolate (54 per cent
cocoa solids), chopped**

1 Preheat the oven to 120°C (235°F/Gas ½). Line a wire rack with baking paper and place over a baking tray.

2 Spread the orange slices on the prepared rack and bake, turning halfway through cooking, for 2½ hours, or until dried but not coloured. Turn off the oven and allow the oranges to cool in the oven.

3 Place the chocolate in a small heatproof bowl over a saucepan of simmering water, ensuring the bowl doesn't touch the water. Stir until the chocolate has melted. Remove from the heat.

4 Line a tray with baking paper. Dip half of each orange slice into the chocolate, tapping gently on the side of the bowl to remove any excess. Place on the prepared tray and stand in a cool place until the chocolate has set.

5 The dried orange slices (without the chocolate) will keep, stored in an airtight container, for up to 1 week. Once dipped in the chocolate they will keep for 1 day.

Meringue kisses with chocolate coffee cream

MAKES 20

COFFEE CREAM
2 egg whites
¼ teaspoon almond essence
115 g (4 oz/½ cup) caster (superfine) sugar

CHOCOLATE COFFEE CREAM
200 g (7 oz) dark chocolate, chopped
1 tablespoon instant coffee granules
125 ml (4 fl oz/½ cup) cream, for whipping

1 Preheat the oven to 150°C (300°F/Gas 2). Line two baking trays with baking paper.

2 Place the egg whites in a large bowl and beat using electric beaters until firm peaks form. Mix in the almond essence, then add sugar, a spoonful at a time, and beat until sugar has dissolved and mixture is thick and glossy.

3 Transfer meringue mixture to a piping (icing) bag fitted with a 1 cm (½ inch) plain nozzle and pipe rounds at 3 cm (1¼ inch) intervals, allowing room for spreading, onto prepared trays. Or, place teaspoons of mixture, spacing them well apart, on the prepared trays. Bake for 45 minutes. Turn off the oven and leave the door slightly ajar, allowing the meringues to cool slowly. **»**

4 To make the chocolate coffee cream, place chocolate, coffee and cream in a heatproof bowl over a saucepan of simmering water, ensuring the bowl doesn't touch the water. Stir until chocolate has melted and mixture is smooth. Cool, cover with plastic wrap and refrigerate until required.

5 Use the chocolate coffee cream to sandwich the meringues together.

6 These filled meringues are best eaten immediately. Unfilled meringues will keep, stored in an airtight container, for up to 2 weeks.

Chocolate caramel tartlets

MAKES 42

200 g (7 oz) dark chocolate, chopped
30 g (1 oz) unsalted butter, cubed

TART CASES
110 g (3¾ oz) plain (all-purpose) flour
½ teaspoon baking powder
90 g (3¼ oz/1 cup) desiccated coconut
95 g (3¼ oz/½ cup) soft brown sugar
125 g (4½ oz/½ cup) unsalted butter, melted
1 teaspoon natural vanilla extract

CARAMEL FILLING
395 g (14 oz) tin sweetened condensed milk
95 g (3½ oz/½ cup) soft brown sugar
80 g (2¾ oz) unsalted butter, cubed
2 tablespoons golden syrup (light treacle)

1 Preheat the oven to 180°C (350°F/Gas 4).
Grease 42 holes of four 12-hole mini muffin tins. **»**

2 To make the tart cases, sift the flour and baking powder into a medium-sized bowl, add the coconut and sugar and stir with a wooden spoon. Stir in the butter and vanilla until combined. Divide mixture evenly among the prepared tins, pressing firmly into the bases and sides. Bake for 12 minutes, or until light golden and crisp.

3 To make caramel filling, combine condensed milk, sugar, butter and the golden syrup in a heavy-based saucepan over low heat and stir until the sugar has dissolved. Bring to a simmer and cook, stirring constantly, for 5 minutes, or until caramel mixture darkens slightly.

4 Immediately spoon the caramel filling into the tartlet cases. Bake for 5–8 minutes, or until caramel is bubbling around the edges. Allow to cool in tins for 10 minutes, then use a small spatula to transfer tartlets to a wire rack to cool completely.

5 To make the chocolate topping, combine the chocolate and butter in a heatproof bowl over a saucepan of simmering water, ensuring the bowl doesn't touch the water. Stir until chocolate and butter have melted. Remove from heat. Spread a thick layer of chocolate evenly over the top of the tartlets. Stand in a cool place for 4–6 hours, or until the chocolate has set.

6 These tartlets will keep, stored in an airtight container, for up to 2 weeks.

Real chocolate crackles

MAKES 36

75 g (2¾ oz/2½ cups) puffed rice cereal
90 g (3¼ oz/1 cup) desiccated coconut
250 g (9 oz) dark chocolate (54 per cent cocoa solids), chopped
icing (confectioners') sugar, sifted, for dusting (optional)

1 Line three 12-hole mini muffin tins with paper cases.

2 Combine the puffed rice and coconut in a large bowl. Place the chocolate in a heatproof bowl over a saucepan of simmering water, ensuring the bowl doesn't touch the water. Stir until the chocolate has melted. Remove from the heat. **»**

3 Add the melted chocolate to the puffed rice mixture and, using a wooden spoon, stir gently until evenly combined. Spoon the mixture into the paper cases. Place in the refrigerator for 1 hour, or until set. Dust with the icing sugar if desired.

4 The chocolate crackles will keep, stored in an airtight container placed in the refrigerator, for up to 2 weeks.

TIP You can also make delicate, bite-sized chocolate crackles to serve after dinner with coffee. Use 72 confectionery chocolate cases instead of mini muffin paper cases.

White chocolate and lime truffles

MAKES 36

80 ml (2½ fl oz/⅓ cup) thickened
(whipping) cream
600 g (1 lb 5 oz) white chocolate, chopped
3 teaspoons finely grated lime zest
lime zest strips, to decorate

1 Place cream and half the chocolate in a heatproof bowl over a saucepan of simmering water, ensuring the bowl doesn't touch the water. Stir until chocolate has melted. Remove from heat, add the grated zest, cover and chill for 30 minutes.

2 Grease a 17 cm (6½ inch) square cake tin and line the base and sides with baking paper. Line a tray with baking paper.

3 Beat chocolate mixture using electric beaters for 3 minutes. Spoon into prepared tin and smooth the surface with the back of a spoon. Chill for 2 hours, or until firm.

4 Turn out the chocolate mixture onto a cutting board. Trim the edges, then cut into 2.5 cm (1 inch) squares. Transfer the squares to the prepared tray. Freeze for 20 minutes. »

5 Meanwhile, place the remaining chocolate in a heatproof bowl over a saucepan of simmering water, ensuring the bowl doesn't touch the water. Stir until the chocolate has melted. Remove from the heat.

6 Using two forks, dip the chocolate squares, one at a time, into the melted chocolate, allowing any excess to drip off. Return to the tray, immediately place a strip of lime zest on each square and stand in a cool place until the chocolate has set.

7 These truffles will keep, stored in a single layer in an airtight container in a cool place, for up to 2 days.

Hazelnut and chocolate meringue fingers

MAKES 12

100 g (3½ oz) hazelnuts, toasted and skinned
4 egg whites, at room temperature
pinch of salt
230 g (8 oz/1 cup) caster (superfine) sugar
60 g (2¼ oz) dark chocolate (54 per cent
cocoa solids), chopped
10 g (¼ oz) unsalted butter, cubed
cream to serve (optional)

CHOCOLATE GANACHE
150 g (5½ oz) dark chocolate (54 per cent
cocoa solids), chopped
125 ml (4 fl oz/½ cup) cream
1½ tablespoons Frangelico

1 Preheat the oven to 100°C (200°F/Gas ½).
Draw two 12 x 20 cm (4½ x 8 inch) rectangles each
on three pieces of baking paper and place on three
baking trays, with the pencil marks facing down.

2 Place the hazelnuts in the bowl of a food processor
and process until finely ground. »

3 Beat the egg whites and salt in a large bowl using electric beaters until soft peaks form. Add the sugar, a spoonful at a time, and beat until very thick and glossy and all the sugar has dissolved. Use a large metal spoon or spatula to fold the ground hazelnuts into the meringue mixture. Divide meringue evenly among the marked rectangles on the prepared trays and use the back of a spoon to spread out evenly. Bake, rotating the trays every 20 minutes, for 1 hour, or until crisp. Turn off the oven and leave meringue rectangles in the oven for 2 hours, or until cooled to room temperature.

4 Meanwhile, to make the chocolate ganache, combine chocolate and cream in a small saucepan over low heat and stir until the chocolate has melted. Stir in the Frangelico, and then set aside to cool to a thin, spreadable consistency.

5 Spread half the chocolate ganache over two of the meringue rectangles. Top each with another meringue rectangle, spread on remaining ganache and finish with a layer of meringue, to form two meringue stacks. Cover with plastic wrap and place the stacks in the refrigerator for 30 minutes, or until ganache is firm.

6 Place the chocolate and butter in a heatproof bowl over a saucepan of simmering water, ensuring the bowl doesn't touch the water. Stir until the chocolate has melted. **»**

7 Carefully transfer the meringue stacks to a cutting board. Use a sharp knife to cut each stack into six slices. Drizzle with chocolate and butter mixture and stand at room temperature for at least 30 minutes.

8 Serve accompanied by the cream, if desired.

TIP Hazelnut meringues with chocolate ganache will keep, stored in an airtight container at room temperature, for up to 2 days.

Chocolate orange fudge

MAKES 36 PIECES

**395 g (13¾ oz) tin sweetened
condensed milk
50 g (1¾ oz) unsalted butter, cubed
200 g (7 oz) orange-flavoured dark
chocolate, finely chopped
200 g (7 oz) dark chocolate (54 per cent
cocoa solids), finely chopped**

1 Line base and sides of an 18 cm (7 inch) square cake tin with baking paper, extending the paper over two opposite sides for easy removal later.

2 Place the condensed milk and butter in a heavy-based saucepan and cook over low heat, stirring occasionally, until the butter has melted. Bring just to a simmer, stirring frequently. Remove from the heat and set aside for 5 minutes to cool slightly. Add both types of the chocolate and stir until the chocolate has melted. **»**

3 Working quickly, pour the fudge mixture into the prepared tin and use the back of a metal spoon to smooth the surface. Place in the refrigerator for 4 hours, or until firm.

4 Remove the fudge from the tin and cut into 3 cm (1¼ inch) squares.

5 This fudge will keep, with the layers separated by baking paper, stored in an airtight container in the refrigerator, for up to 1 month.

TIP Don't use orange-flavoured chocolate with a soft or liquid centre.

Chocolate and pecan honey wafers

MAKES ABOUT 25 PIECES

35 g (1¼ oz) plain (all-purpose) flour
25 g (1 oz) caster (superfine) sugar
85 g (3 oz) honey (such as iron bark or blue gum), warmed slightly
65 g (2½ oz) unsalted butter, melted and cooled
1 egg white
70 g (2½ oz) dark chocolate, roughly chopped
70 g (2½ oz) pecans, roughly chopped

1 Preheat the oven to 160°C (315°F/Gas 2–3). Line two baking trays with baking paper.

2 Combine the flour, sugar, honey, butter and egg white in the bowl of a food processor and process until just combined. Divide the mixture between the baking trays and spread with the back of a spoon to form two thin 20 x 25 cm (8 x 10 inch) rectangles of equal thickness. Sprinkle evenly with the chocolate and pecans. »

3 Bake, swapping the trays halfway through cooking, for 24–28 minutes, or until dark golden. Allow to cool on the trays.

4 Break into pieces roughly 5 cm (2 inch) and serve.

5 These wafers will keep, stored in an airtight container, for up to 1 week.

Chocolate peanut butter cups

MAKES 20

300 g (10½ oz) dark chocolate (54 per cent
cocoa solids), chopped
125 g (4½ oz/½ cup) smooth or crunchy
peanut butter
30 g (1 oz /¼ cup) icing
(confectioners') sugar
40 g (1½ oz/¼ cup) roasted unsalted
peanuts, chopped

1 Place 220 g (7¾ oz) of the chocolate in a heatproof bowl over a saucepan of simmering water, ensuring the bowl doesn't touch the water. Stir until the chocolate has melted. Remove from the heat. Divide the chocolate among 20 small fluted foil cases, using a teaspoon to spread the chocolate evenly up the sides to form a thin layer. Set aside for 20 minutes, or until the chocolate has cooled slightly. **»**

2 Meanwhile, place the remaining 80 g (2¾ oz) of chocolate in a heatproof bowl over a saucepan of simmering water, ensuring the bowl doesn't touch the water. Stir until the chocolate has melted. Remove from the heat. Stir in the peanut butter and sugar. Spoon the filling into a piping (icing) bag fitted with a 1 cm (½ inch) plain nozzle. Pipe the filling into the chocolate cups. Top each cup with the chopped peanuts and set aside in a cool place for 1 hour, or until the filling firms slightly.

3 These chocolate cups will keep, stored in an airtight container, for up to 1 week.

Turkish delight and pistachio rocky road

MAKES ABOUT 36 PIECES

400 g (14 oz) dark chocolate (54 per cent
cocoa solids), chopped
110 g (3¾ oz) Turkish delight, cubed
60 g (2¼ oz/1 cup) shredded coconut
100 g (3½ oz/¾ cup) pistachio nuts, lightly
toasted and coarsely chopped
icing (confectioners') sugar, sifted, for
dusting (optional)

1 Line the base and long sides of a 16 x 26 cm
(6¼ x 10½ inch) baking tin with baking paper,
allowing the paper to overhang the sides.

2 Place the chocolate in a heatproof bowl over a
saucepan of simmering water, ensuring the bowl
doesn't touch the water. Stir until the chocolate has
melted. Remove from the heat and set aside, stirring
occasionally, to cool to room temperature. »

3 Add the Turkish delight, coconut and pistachio nuts to the cooled chocolate and stir to combine. Spoon into the prepared tin and use the back of the spoon to spread evenly. Lightly tap the tin on the bench to settle the mixture. Stand in a cool place for 1–4 hours, or until the chocolate has set (this will depend on the weather).

4 Transfer the rocky road to a cutting board. Use a 3 cm (1¼ inch) cookie cutter dipped in cornflour to cut into rounds. Dust with the sugar, if desired, and place in small paper cases to serve.

5 These rocky road bites will keep, stored in an airtight container in a cool place, for up to 1 month.

Milk chocolate and cashew truffles

MAKES ABOUT 18

150 g (5½ oz) milk chocolate, chopped
60 ml (2 fl oz/¼ cup) cream (whipping)
1 tablespoon Kahlua or Tia Maria
60 g (2¼ oz) unsalted cashew nuts, lightly
toasted and finely chopped

1 Place the chocolate and cream in a heatproof bowl over a saucepan of simmering water, ensuring the bowl doesn't touch the water. Stir until the chocolate has melted. Remove from the heat and stir in the liqueur. Cover with plastic wrap and transfer to the refrigerator for 1–2 hours, stirring occasionally, or until the mixture is firm enough to roll into balls.

2 Spread the cashew nuts on a plate. Roll small teaspoons of the chocolate mixture into balls, then roll in the cashew nuts to coat. Place the finished truffles in paper cases, if desired, transfer to a plate and return to the refrigerator for at least 1 hour before serving.

3 These truffles will keep, stored in an airtight container in the refrigerator, for up to 2 weeks.

Individual chocolate, date and walnut tortes

MAKES 8

vegetable oil, to grease
4 egg whites, at room temperature
80 g (2¾ oz/⅓ cup) caster (superfine) sugar
150 g (5½ oz) dark chocolate (54 per cent
cocoa solids), chopped
150 g (5½ oz/1½ cups) walnut
halves, chopped
120 g (4¼ oz/⅔ cup) pitted dates, chopped
1 tablespoon unsweetened cocoa
powder, sifted
cream, lightly whipped, to serve

1 Preheat the oven to 160°C (315°F/Gas 2–3). Brush eight 8 cm (3¼ inch) loose-based fluted flan (tart) tins with oil and line the bases with rounds of baking paper. Place the tins on a baking tray. **»**

2 Beat the egg whites in a large bowl using electric beaters until soft peaks begin to form. Add sugar, a tablespoon at a time, and beat until thick and glossy.

3 Use a large metal spoon or spatula to fold the chocolate, the walnuts, the dates and the cocoa into the meringue mixture. Divide the mixture among the prepared tins and smooth the surfaces with the back of a spoon. Bake for 40 minutes, or until the tortes start to pull away slightly from the edge of the tins. Turn off the oven and allow the tortes to cool in the oven with the door slightly ajar.

4 Remove the tortes from the tins and transfer to serving plates. Serve accompanied by the cream.

TIP These tortes will keep, stored in an airtight container, for up to 2 days.

Chocolate hazelnut wheels

MAKES 16

100 g (3½ oz) unsalted butter, softened
55 g (2 oz/¼ cup) caster (superfine) sugar
1 egg, at room temperature
125 g (4½ oz/1 cup) plain (all-purpose) flour
30 g (1 oz/¼ cup) unsweetened
cocoa powder
55 g (2 oz/½ cup) ground hazelnuts
70 g (2½ oz/½ cup) hazelnuts, toasted,
skinned and chopped

CHOCOLATE FILLING
100 g (3½ oz) dark chocolate (54 per cent
cocoa solids), chopped
50 g (1¾ oz) butter, softened
40 g (1½ oz/⅓ cup) icing (confectioners')
sugar, sifted

1 Beat the butter and sugar in a large bowl using electric beaters until just combined, then add the egg, beating until just combined. Sift in the flour and the cocoa, add ground hazelnuts and, using a wooden spoon, stir to form a soft dough. Shape into a flat disc, cover with plastic wrap and refrigerate for 30 minutes. »

2 Preheat the oven to 180°C (350°F/Gas 4). Line two baking trays with baking paper.

3 Roll out the dough on a lightly floured work surface until 5 mm (¼ inch) thick. Chill for 30 minutes, then cut the dough into 32 rounds using a 5 cm (2 inch) cookie cutter, re-rolling the dough when necessary. Place on the prepared trays, then refrigerate for 10 minutes.

4 Bake, swapping the trays halfway through cooking, for 15 minutes, or until biscuits are cooked through and aromatic. Allow to cool completely on the trays.

5 Meanwhile, to make chocolate filling, place the chocolate in a heatproof bowl over a saucepan of simmering water, ensuring the bowl doesn't touch the water. Stir until chocolate has melted. Set aside to cool to room temperature. Beat the cooled, melted chocolate and butter using electric beaters until creamy. Add sugar and beat until well combined.

6 Use the chocolate filling to sandwich the biscuits together, spreading the filling around the sides of the sandwiched biscuits. Roll the biscuit sides in the chopped hazelnuts.

7 Filled biscuits will keep, stored in an airtight container, for up to 5 days. Unfilled biscuits will keep, stored in an airtight container, for up to 2 weeks.

White chocolate bark

MAKES ABOUT 50 PIECES

160 g (5¾ oz/1 cup) unsalted macadamia nuts, chopped
225 g (8 oz/1⅔ cups) chopped white chocolate
120 g (4¼ oz/⅔ cup) dried apricots, finely chopped
50 g (1¾ oz/⅓ cup) currants

1 Preheat the oven to 180°C (350°F/Gas 4) and line a baking tray with baking paper.

2 Spread nuts over a second baking tray and toast for 5–6 minutes, or until lightly browned, shaking the tray once or twice to ensure even toasting. Cool. Place chocolate in a heatproof bowl over a saucepan of simmering water, ensuring the bowl doesn't touch the water. Stir until the chocolate is just melted and smooth. Remove from heat, then add two-thirds of the nuts and dried fruit and stir to coat.

3 Pour mixture onto prepared tray and spread to form approximately a square of 25 cm (10 inches). Scatter over the remaining nuts and dried fruit. Cover with plastic wrap and refrigerate until set. Break into 4 -5 cm chunks. Store, in an airtight container, in the refrigerator for 3 weeks.

Chocolate meringues

MAKES 24

2 egg whites, at room temperature
pinch of salt
115 g (4 oz/½ cup) caster (superfine) sugar
75 g (2¾ oz) dark chocolate (70 per cent
cocoa solids), coarsely grated
unsweetened cocoa powder, sifted, for
dusting (optional)

1 Preheat the oven to 120°C (235°F/Gas ½). Line two baking trays with baking paper.

2 Beat the egg whites and salt in a medium bowl using electric beaters until soft peaks form. Add the sugar, a spoonful at a time, and beat until the sugar has dissolved, the mixture is thick and glossy and a long trailing peak forms when the beater is lifted. Use a large metal spoon to fold in the chocolate.

3 Spoon large teaspoonfuls of the mixture onto the prepared trays about 2 cm (¾ inch) apart. Dust with cocoa, if desired. Place meringues in the oven and immediately reduce temperature to 100°C (200°F/Gas ½). Bake for 1½ hours, or until the meringues are crisp and sound hollow when tapped on base. Turn the oven off, leaving the door slightly ajar and leave the meringues to cool slowly.

4 These meringues will keep, stored in an airtight container, for up to 1 week

Published in 2012 by Murdoch Books Pty Limited

Publisher: Anneka Manning
Editor: Liz Malcolm
Designer: Adam Walker

For Corporate Orders & Custom Publishing contact Noel Hammond,
National Business Development Manager Murdoch Books Australia

Text and photography © Murdoch Books Pty Limited 2008.
Design © Murdoch Books Pty Limited 2012.

A cataloguing-in-publication entry is available from the catalogue
of the National Library of Australia at www.nla.gov.au.

A catalogue record for this book is available from the British Library.

Printed by Toppan Leefung Printing Limited, China

Murdoch Books Australia
Pier 8/9
23 Hickson Road
Millers Point NSW 2000
Phone: +61 (0) 2 8220 2000
Fax: +61 (0) 2 8220 2558
www.murdochbooks.com.au
info@murdochbooks.com.au

Murdoch Books UK Limited
Erico House, 6th Floor
93–99 Upper Richmond Road
Putney, London SW15 2TG
Phone: +44 (0) 20 8785 5995
Fax: +44 (0) 20 8785 5985
www.murdochbooks.co.uk
info@murdochbooks.co.uk

IMPORTANT: Those who might be at risk from the effects of salmonella poisoning (the elderly,
pregnant women, young children and those suffering from immune deficiency diseases) should
consult their doctor with any concerns about eating raw eggs.

OVEN GUIDE: You may find cooking times vary depending on the oven you are using.
For fan-forced ovens, as a general rule, set the oven temperature to 20°C (35°F) lower than
indicated in the recipe.

We have used 20 ml (4 teaspoon) tablespoon measures. If you are using a 15 ml (3 teaspoon)
tablespoon add an extra teaspoon of the ingredient for each tablespoon specified.